THE
Bride's
Book
OF
IDEAS

THE Bride's Book OF IDEAS

by

MARJORIE PALMER

and

ETHEL BOWMAN

TYNDALE HOUSE PUBLISHERS, INC. WHEATON, ILLINOIS

First printing, revised edition, March 1985
Library of Congress Catalog Card Number 84-52260
ISBN 0-8423-0180-1
Printed in the United States of America

*Dedicated
to our daughters,*
PAULA,
BONNIE,
and
JAN

CONTENTS

A Special Word to Brides

PREFACE
by Marge Palmer

I will bless the Lord who counsels me; he gives me wisdom in the night. He tells me what to do.
PSALM 16:7

You are married now.

You have just taken the name of the most wonderful man in the world and are happier than you have ever thought possible.

You are sure of many things about your marriage. It isn't going to turn sour and commonplace. The years will be vibrant and alive, exciting adventures of love. Christ is going to have first place in your home. The spiritual roots will be deep and strong. You are going to keep your home what it ought to be by being a sweet, agreeable, efficient wife and homemaker.

But marriage isn't like the honeymoon. You have to clean and wash and cook. You may have to shop on a budget that never seems to stretch quite far enough. Perhaps you have a job, as well. Even if you've been on your own for a while, putting together a new, two-person household presents infinite complications. It's all new and a little frightening.

I can still remember my frustration and bewilderment when I was faced with these responsibilities for the first time. They came to mind again when our oldest daughter was married and began to keep house. I thought about them as I helped Bonnie struggle through her first "company" dinner and later as she came to me with the problems of shopping and cooking.

It was Bonnie who saw the need for a bride's handbook. I had taught her to clean and sew and cook, but she felt she needed something more, a practical handbook giving help for many of the problems facing an inexperienced young homemaker.

"Why doesn't somebody write a book telling us the sort of things you're helping me with now?" she asked.

This is the result.

We have included a wide variety of tasty but simple and inexpensive recipes, and information you will need about shopping, food preparation, entertaining, and homemaking.

You will want to keep this book within easy reach in your kitchen. It contains the answers to many of the homemaking problems that will

9

frustrate and upset you during the first bewildering months of housekeeping. Using it should help make you a gracious hostess and a better, more efficient wife.

GETTING OFF TO A GOOD START

Planning Your Life Together

ONE

PRECEPTS FOR A HAPPY HOME

Many couples speak of arguments and quarrels as though they cannot be avoided, as though every marriage must have its share of fights. That isn't the way God intended marriage to be. He ordained it to be happy, ruled by love for him and for each other. He compares marriage to the relationship between the Church and the Lord Jesus Christ—an enduring institution born and nurtured in love.

While God sets down the precepts that will make your marriage happy and purposeful, he does not force his will upon you. He tells you how to achieve perfect harmony in your marriage, but you will have to seek it actively.

The precepts for a happy home are few and simple.

Be content with what you have. Materialism is a common ailment today, even among Christians, and it is easy to get into debt. Refrigerators, cars, television sets, home furnishings, washers, and dryers can all be bought on credit cards. While credit buying has become a part of our way of life and can serve a useful purpose, it is easy to burden yourself with so many debts that you will have difficulty paying your bills. When that happens, discord is not far behind.

If you feel that you must buy a certain item, sit down first and count the cost. Examine your entire financial situation critically and be sure you can make the additional payments without trouble.

Make a habit of saving regularly. Emergencies have a way of popping up when you can least afford them. Prepare ahead of time and you will find the emergency much less serious.

Treat your husband with courtesy and respect and expect the same treatment from him. You are both individuals with different personalities, feelings, and needs. Don't take advantage of the love your husband has for you and give way to your own anger and frustration. The home is the most important place to practice the Golden Rule.

The wise man is glad to be instructed. . . .
PROVERBS 10:8

Treat your husband as you would like him to treat you. This can set up a chain reaction that will keep your married life sweet and harmonious.

If you can settle the little problems of daily living without bickering, you will find it much easier to solve more serious problems.

Remember that your husband is the head of the house. Some brides resent what they view as a subordinate role and are determined not to allow this "antiquated" precept to have any place in their lives. But God charges the husband with the responsibility for making major decisions and being the spiritual leader of the home.

It may not be easy for you to accept this, but I can assure you from my own experience of more than twenty-five years of marriage, and from observing countless other couples, that it is often the key to a happy marriage.

The fact that your husband is given the position of authority in your home does not mean that he has automatic and complete control over you. God establishes the limits of your husband's authority and tempers it with responsibility and love.

My husband says I have taken my rightful place according to the biblical injunction, yet I don't feel that I am anybody's slave. It has been comforting and reassuring to have someone to lean upon, someone to trust to take care of me and our family.

Don't let disagreements and differences go unresolved. The Bible warns against letting the sun go down upon our wrath. And with good reason. Minor resentments and disagreements can grow in size if they are allowed to build. Who is right and who is wrong isn't important when compared to the harm that discord can work.

One person can't carry on a quarrel alone. Remember this the next time an argument threatens. It isn't easy to say, "I'm sorry." It isn't easy to hold your tongue against the fire of anger. Yet you and your husband must do so if your life together is going to be peaceful and happy.

Give the Lord his rightful place in your marriage. Newly married couples can be so concerned with one another that they neglect the Lord. Their church attendance may become sporadic and their Bible reading and time of prayer indifferent and meaningless.

If you want God's help in making your marriage successful, you must give your lives completely to him. Attend Sunday school and church services regularly and have a regular time of Bible reading and prayer each day. If you get into the habit of taking your smaller problems and needs to God in prayer, you will naturally turn to him when the more important matters come up.

Don't hide your light! Let it shine for all; let your good deeds glow for all to see, so that they will praise your heavenly Father.
MATTHEW 5:15, 16

Love forgets mistakes; nagging about them parts the best of friends.
PROVERBS 17:9

If you practice these precepts your marriage will be happy and will bring honor and glory to God. Those who know you will be envious of the joy you have and covet it for themselves. Your marriage will be truly successful by God's standards as well as your own.

COMMITMENT

Webster defines commitment as: The act of committing; a *giving* in charge or entrusting; the act of referring a legislative bill to committee; *something pledged,* an engagement by contract involving financial obligation; the state of being bound emotionally or intellectually to a course of action.

"Many waters cannot quench the flame of love, neither can the floods drown it. If a man tried to buy it with everything he owned, he couldn't do it."
SONG OF
SOLOMON 8:7

The subject of commitment came up as I chatted with a friend over a cup of coffee recently. She confided, "Frankly, Jim and I have been having serious problems in our marriage." As she went into detail, I recognized problems dealing with finances, children, and other more complex problems as ones that my husband and I had also faced. This being a second marriage for both of them, divorce was definitely an option—a very real option.

As we talked, she established the fact that she really did want this marriage to work. That last word struck me as being one key to marriages that do work. I asked her if she was really willing to work at the marriage. Startled, she said that she was, of course, but that she couldn't do it alone.

Then I asked her what she would do if she had no other choices. If somehow she, along with her Jim, would *have* to make it work. Puzzled, she asked me what I meant.

I explained that some years ago now, my husband and I had made a very serious commitment to each other after some years of marriage. We actually made a ninety-nine-year commitment. This simply meant that instead of running away from problems, we had to face them—head on—and work them out.

We had made a commitment. This actually gave a whole new outlook on the marriage. It meant that sometimes I would spend hours in prayer, asking God to help me to love my husband in the way that he would have me to love him—or—to help *him* love me in spite of my sometimes unloving ways. God has answered those prayers over and over again.

She agreed to talk to her husband after praying about it first. I agreed to pray for her and for him, too. It is God's desire that we have strong, loving homes. He can help and really wants to and will bless us if we'll only give him a chance.

TOGETHERNESS

"Talk with each other much about the Lord, quoting psalms and hymns and singing sacred songs, making music in your hearts to the Lord.

"Always give thanks for everything to our God and Father in the name of our Lord Jesus Christ.

"Honor Christ by submitting to each other.

"You wives must submit to your husbands' leadership in the same way you submit to the Lord. . . .

"And you husbands, show the same kind of love to your wives as Christ showed to the church when he died for her, to make her holy and clean, washed by baptism and God's word; so that he could give her to himself as a glorious church without a single spot or wrinkle or any other blemish, being holy and without a single fault.

"That is how husbands should treat their wives, loving them as parts of themselves. For since a man and his wife are now one, a man is really doing himself a favor and loving himself when he loves his wife! No one hates his own body but lovingly cares for it, just as Christ cares for his body the church, of which we are parts.

"(That the husband and wife are one body is proved by the Scripture which says, 'A man must leave his father and mother when he marries, so that he can be perfectly joined to his wife, and the two shall be one.')" *Ephesians 5:19-31*

Kind words are like honey—enjoyable and healthful.
PROVERBS 16:24

FRIENDS

You should have three kinds of friends:

1. Those who are at the same level as you are spiritually, for you can strengthen and encourage each other in the Lord.

2. Those who are closer to God, for they will help you grow in wisdom and spiritual stature.

3. Those who are further from Christ than you, or perhaps aren't even Christians, for you will be able to witness to them and help bring them to Christ.

In your friendship with the unsaved, you must be extremely careful and completely honest with yourself. If your association with them has the tendency to draw them to God, the relationship is sound and has his blessing. If, on the other hand, you find that being with such friends has a tendency to pull you away from Christ or tempts you to do things you know are unbecoming to a Christian, the only wise thing is to avoid a close friendship with them regardless of how much you enjoy their company.

A friendly discussion is as stimulating as the sparks that fly when iron strikes iron.
PROVERBS 27:17

If your foot carries you toward evil, cut it off! Better be lame and live forever than have two feet that carry you to hell.
MARK 9:45, 46

PERSONAL DEVOTIONS

Are you a sleepyhead? Do you like to close your eyes for a few more minutes of sleep after turning off the alarm? If that's your problem, you undoubtedly find it hard to squeeze in a few minutes of Bible reading and prayer before the activities of the day begin. But someone once said, "As your morning begins, so is your day."

Start each day alone with God and his Word. You will find the frustrations and problems of the day easier to face if you have sought him in the morning. It takes discipline at first to set your alarm fifteen minutes early or to get up when it goes off. But once you have established the habit and have learned what a time alone with God can do for you, you will find it the most rewarding time of your day.

Each morning I will look to you in heaven and lay my requests before you, praying earnestly.
PSALM 5:3

Managing Your Home

A WEEKLY PLAN

Old-fashioned spring and fall cleaning like grandmother used to do? Come spring and fall she drove herself through the hated chore of doing it all in one week. With modern appliances these dreaded cleaning methods are no longer necessary, and many women dispense with the old schedules of "Monday—wash; Tuesday—iron," and so on. Still, it is wise to have some weekly plan of work.

Here's a suggestion: Each week do special cleaning in one room along with your regular cleaning. Concentrate on the bedroom one week. Do the curtains need washing? Are the rugs and bedspreads soiled? How about straightening the closet and removing clothing that doesn't fit anymore? A few minutes with a window cleaner will make windows sparkle. Just doing one or two of these things each day will produce a beautifully clean bedroom by the end of the week, and you will not have exhausted yourself in the process!

The next week concentrate on the kitchen, doing curtains and windows one day, utensil and linen drawers another day, several cabinets the next—and so on through the week. Of course, you will be wiping the cupboards and stove and refrigerator each day as you do the dishes, so that soil does not build up and make the cleaning more difficult later on. Before long, your mother-in-law will be coming to you to learn the secret of your shining, orderly home!

Take particular care not to neglect the corners and out-of-the way places. The habits you set up now will probably be the ones that govern the rest of your life. A clean house makes a healthier, happier family.

If you find things go better if you have a schedule to work by, here is a suggested outline:

Monday. Do laundry. Tidy the house. Clean silverware and straighten utensil drawers.

Tuesday. Iron. Before putting clothes away, sew on missing buttons and do other mending.

She watches carefully all that goes on throughout her household, and is never lazy. Her children stand and bless her; so does her husband. He praises her with these words: "There are many fine women in the world, but you are the best of them all!"
PROVERBS
31:27-29

To remove a broken lightbulb safely, first unplug the lamp or turn off the power. Push a large cork into the broken end. You can now unscrew it easily.

Wednesday. General cleaning. Clean refrigerator.

Thursday. Plan menus for the week to come, and do grocery shopping.

Friday. Clean thoroughly for the weekend.

Saturday. Do baking. Prepare as much of Sunday dinner as possible and press clothing for church. Prepare yourself spiritually for the Lord's Day; review the Sunday school lesson and pray for the pastor and teachers in your church.

Sunday. Be on time to Sunday school and church services. Rest, relax, and read your Bible. Enjoy fellowship with friends or relatives and attend the evening services.

If you have a job, as so many of today's brides do, this schedule must be condensed into after-work hours. Don't try to force a schedule that doesn't fit you, but work out one you can use. A bit of experimenting will produce exactly the right plan for you to keep up with your housework.

I will sing about your lovingkindness and your justice, Lord. I will sing your praises!
PSALM 101:1

SING AS YOU WORK

Can you sing and not be happy? Can you be happy and not sing?

When God delivered the Israelites from the hand of Pharaoh by taking them safely through the Red Sea, Moses and his people sang about the Lord's strength and salvation. Miriam the prophetess did the same. And so did David, whose harp is as well known as his sling. It was David's music that lulled Saul's restless spirit while it echoed David's joy and trust in God. The angels sang as they heralded the birth of Christ.

You, too, should sing as you work around the house, whether you have to fit the cooking and cleaning and washing into the hours left after you have completed a day's work, or whether keeping house is your sole responsibility. Sing songs of praise, of prayer, of service. Sing Bible verses set to music, such as "I know whom I have believed"; "Beloved, now are we the sons of God"; and "The Lord is my Shepherd." You will find that your days are smoother, sweeter, and happier if there is a song in your heart.

Don't withhold repayment of your debts. Don't say "some other time," if you can pay now.
PROVERBS 3:27, 28

MANAGING MONEY

Managing money is undoubtedly one of the most serious problems you and your husband will face. There are so many things you need; so many things you would like to have; so many bills that can't be avoided. Rent, utilities, and groceries all have to be paid for continually.

Few things can sour the happiness of a new marriage quicker than a raft of unpaid accounts and threatening letters from collectors. It is far better not to buy things you don't need than to allow them to box you in and cause disharmony in your home—as most surely they will.

Credit cards and easy-to-open charge accounts must be handled carefully. They can be a great convenience or a terrible curse, depending on the restraint you are able to exercise. Remember, anything you charge has to be paid for. And if you can't pay promptly, the interest charges on such accounts are extremely high.

A Canadian expert on money management worked out a formula for those who come to him for guidance, a formula that might work for you.

To remove scorched spots from clothing, wet the material and place it in direct sunlight. Repeat if necessary.

1. First your tithe, income tax, and social security tax should be taken out of your monthly income.

2. Put 10 percent of the balance into some form of savings.

3. Use 20 percent to apply to old bills or the purchase of new items.

4. Live on the balance.

He claims that the average young couple who follows this formula will be financially independent when they retire.

Whether that formula will work for you is something only you and your husband can decide. However, you should have a plan for regular savings, even though it means postponing the purchase of some items you would like to have.

INSURANCE

If you haven't already had insurance agents call on you, you will. Insurance is a must, for it provides protection that you cannot afford to be without. Yet you must be careful in selecting insurance.

Premiums have a way of sounding easier to pay than they actually are. You may find that the program the agent presents to you is actually such a burden that you might not be able to keep it in force. Having to drop insurance because you cannot pay the premiums means that you are wasting the money you have invested. It is much better to put an insurance program into force slowly and be sure that you can pay the premiums when they fall due.

Some rich people are poor, and some poor people have great wealth!
PROVERBS 13:7

There are certain kinds of insurance that you should not be without. Here are the most important.

1. *Car insurance,* particularly liability insurance. You have a responsibility as a Christian as well as a legal responsibility to see that you have insurance to pay for any accident you might cause. Most states have laws that prohibit a driver involved in an accident from

continuing to drive unless he can furnish proof that he is financially responsible (this means having a bank account or other liquid assets in the amount of thousands of dollars), or proof that he has liability insurance.

2. An ordinary *life insurance* policy of $5,000 for each of you to take care of funeral expenses in the event that the Lord should call one of you to be with him.

3. *Term life insurance* can be bought at a fraction of the cost of ordinary life insurance. While it has no cash value, it provides a maximum amount of coverage for a minimum premium at a time when most couples are just starting out and find it difficult to have the life insurance they should have. If a savings program is wanted in addition to life insurance, that can be done through a bank with a far greater return than an ordinary life policy or an annuity.

4. Adequate *hospitalization insurance* with good maternity benefits. Don't take the agent's word for the benefits; read them in the policy yourself. Your employer may offer a hospitalization plan or you may have the opportunity to join Blue Cross and Blue Shield, which is excellent coverage.

5. *Fire insurance* for household furnishings and personal belongings.

6. *Term insurance* covering all loans including that on your car. This is very inexpensive and means that the indebtedness would be paid if the head of the household dies.

CHOOSING A FAMILY DOCTOR

Choosing a doctor is not always easy when you move to a new community. It is something that should be done with care before the need arises. Although you are healthy now, you never know when you or your husband may have an accident or an emergency that makes it imperative for you to get a doctor immediately. You should know whom to call if such an event happens.

You might want to ask your or your husband's family doctor for a recommendation. One of them might know a competent general practitioner in the city where you will be living. You would have confidence in such a man. If a family doctor cannot help you, talk with the pastor of the church you are attending, or ask your employer or friends in whom you have confidence to suggest a doctor.

FIRST AID

Asphyxiation. Get patient to fresh air. Send for physician. Start rescue breathing at once.

Let us praise the Lord together, and exalt his name. For I cried to him and he answered me. He freed me from all my fears.
PSALM 34:3, 4

Bites, animal. Wash wound thoroughly with soap under running water. Rinse. Call physician.

Bleeding. Press sterile gauze pad firmly against wound until bleeding stops. If you are unable to stop it, call doctor.

Burns. For a slight burn, immerse in cold water or hold under cold running water for 2 or 3 minutes. If burn is severe, send for physician immediately. Do not attempt treatment.

Choking. The Heimlich Maneuver is usually very effective. Grasp victim from behind with both arms. Make a fist with one hand and place it against the diaphragm, placing the other hand on top. With a quick upward thrust, force trapped air out of the lungs to expel foreign object.

Cuts. Wash small cuts with soap under warm water. Apply antiseptic and bandage. Do not use antiseptic on severe wounds; stop the bleeding, then consult doctor.

Electric Shock. Do not, under any circumstances, try to dislodge the victim from the electrical contact until you have turned off the electricity at the main switch at the fuse box. (If you touch him while the electricity is still on, the current will be conducted through his body into yours, and there will be two victims instead of one!) If it is absolutely impossible to turn off the main switch, it may be necessary to attempt to drag the victim away from the contact by using a rope or loop of dry cloth. *This is dangerous* and it would be well to try to get help before attempting this. When patient is free, call doctor or police rescue unit. If breathing has stopped, use mouth-to-mouth resuscitation until professional help arrives.

Eyes. To remove foreign matter or liquids from eye, have patient lie down at once. Pour water directly into the eye, letting it run off until the matter is removed. If object is imbedded, take patient to physician immediately. Never rub the eye as it may push object deeper.

Fainting. Have patient sit down and lower head to knees. If he doesn't respond, lay him flat on floor with hips raised. Loosen tight clothing. When patient recovers, keep him still for 15 or 20 minutes longer. If he remains unconscious for more than a few minutes, call your doctor.

Falls or accidents. If there is severe pain, *don't* try to move patient. Stop severe bleeding, keep him warm and comfortable until emergency unit arrives.

Poisoning. Call doctor, informing him of what was swallowed. If the container is available, use antidote as recommended there. Induce vomiting only on doctor's orders or if the antidote printed on the container label specifically recommends it.

Any cleaning fluid will remove marks left on skin by adhesive tape.

Rescue breathing. When a person cannot breathe for himself due to electric shock, drowning, or asphyxiation, do the following at once:

1. Tilt head back with patient on back, front of neck stretched.
2. Lift his jaw upward.
3. If air passage is not cleared, clear at once with sharp blows between shoulder blades.
4. Open your mouth wide and cover patient's mouth completely by placing your mouth over his with *airtight* contact, closing patient's nose by pinching it with your thumb and finger.
5. Blow air forcefully into patient's lungs until you see the chest rise (gently for children); remove your mouth and let him exhale. If chest does not rise, repeat steps above.
6. Repeat step 5 twelve times a minute until patient revives (twenty times a minute for children).

Come before him with thankful hearts. Let us sing him psalms of praise.
PSALM 95:2

C.P.R. In most areas C.P.R. (cardiopulmonary resuscitation) classes are given several times a year. This is a very good program on life-saving technique and costs very little. If you watch the papers or check with your local Red Cross you can learn when they will be held. You would be wise to take part in such a program.

Emergency phone numbers. There is a 911 or other emergency phone number in most communities. The number will be found in the front of your phone book. Circle it or write it on the cover so it can be quickly found in case of an emergency.

Be quick, but be calm and specific in describing the emergency. Identify it as a burn, broken limb, fainting, choking, or heart attack. This will greatly help in getting proper equipment immediately and to prepare for quick aid. Be sure and give your name, phone number, and the location of the emergency. Often minutes can make the difference between life and death.

Remove blood and chocolate stains with cool water before washing in hot water. Use detergent and rub gently.

In most areas, there is also a poison control center with a number that can be called night or day. It, too, can usually be found inside the front cover of your telephone book.

If you forget those numbers or can't locate them, dial 0. The operator will help you in case of an emergency.

Setting Up Housekeeping

THREE

KITCHEN AND HOUSEHOLD ESSENTIALS

You probably had a number of showers and received a variety of wedding gifts. You will be more than thankful for all of them as you begin to buy the things you need to set up housekeeping. Fortunately, many of these miscellaneous necessities are inexpensive.

We have listed here the items we find necessary to have in our own kitchens. There may be some you will want to omit and others you will want to add.

Friendly suggestions are as pleasant as perfume.
PROVERBS 27:9

Staples

Salt	Vanilla	Rice	Paper towels
Pepper	Baking powder	Biscuit mix	Matches
Mustard	Baking soda	Cake mixes	Toothpicks
Cinnamon	Shortening	Crackers	Bread
Chili powder	Salad oil	Coffee	Butter or margarine
Sugar	Flour	Tea	Milk
Brown sugar	Vinegar	Aluminum foil	Catsup
Powdered sugar	Spaghetti	Waxed paper	Eggs
Cocoa	Macaroni	Paper napkins	Gelatin

To remove grime from shirt collars, rub liquid shampoo on the collar before laundering.

Housekeeping Aids

Broom	Hot pads	Bowl cleaner	Household deodor-izer
Dust cloth	Dishcloths	Laundry soap	
Sponges	Scouring powder	Liquid detergent	Furniture polish
Dish drainer	Dust mop	Ironing board	Spray starch
Dustpan	Dish towels	Steel wool pads	

An envelope from which a corner has been snipped makes a handy funnel to fill salt shakers.

Utensils

Rolling pin	Dishpan	Teapot	Baking pans
Knives	Can opener	Skillets	Cake pans
Bottle opener	Potato peeler	Cutting board	Pie pans
Pancake turner	Grater	Strainer	Cookie sheets
Flour sifter	Measuring spoons and cups	Long-handled fork	Muffin tins
Mixing bowls		Vegetable brush	Teakettle
Potato masher	Wooden spoons	Rotary egg beater	Salt and pepper shakers
Coffeepot	Saucepans	Spatula	

To scour sharp knives with a cleaning pad, lay the knife on a flat surface and do one side at a time.

Electrical Appliances

Mixer	Toaster	Blender
Covered frying pan	Coffee maker	Waffle iron
Iron	Slow cooker	Can opener

Nice to have, but not essential

Angel-cake pan	Microwave oven	Food processor	Colander
Covered cake pan	Meat and candy	Jell-O molds	Pressure cooker
Kitchen timer	thermometers	Knife sharpener	Popcorn popper
Roasting pan	Food chopper	Griddle	

Toiletries

Soap	Deodorant	Dental floss
Cotton balls	Toothpaste	Shampoo
Bathroom tissue	Facial tissue	Cotton swabs

The Medicine Chest

Antiseptic	Vaseline	BandAids
Antiseptic	Aspirin	
mouthwash	Thermometer	

Always save the tags describing fabrics and giving washing instructions for new garments.

Major Appliances

Unless you and your husband have a higher income than the average young married couple it may be wise for you to consider buying a used refrigerator and stove or renting an apartment where they are furnished.

Most apartments have washing and drying facilities, but if your apartment doesn't, laundromats are so accessible and inexpensive you can probably forego the purchase of a washer and dryer until you have a family. Then the amount of washing you will have and the increased demands on your time will make the use of a laundromat impractical. You will probably want to get your own vacuum cleaner as soon as possible.

Most young couples would say a television set is a necessity. While you may find an expensive color set tempting, you can get a good black and white TV for a fraction of the price you would have to pay for color. Don't overlook the possibility of buying a good used set.

Most wives would enjoy having a new stove with a self-cleaning oven, a freezer or refrigerator that doesn't need defrosting, a washer, a dryer, a dishwasher, and a host of other new and wonderful developments to make housekeeping easier. Trouble can come, however,

A wise man thinks ahead; a fool doesn't, and even brags about it!
PROVERBS 13:16

if you and your husband must buy too much on your credit cards and overextend yourselves.

One way of avoiding too many payments is to limit yourself to one credit purchase at a time. Another is to find a banker you have confidence in and seek his counsel before you make any credit purchase. He not only will be able to give you sound financial advice, but his bank may be able to save you money through its time payment department.

REMOVING SPOTS AND STAINS

Trouble with ironing? A scorched spot on a shirt may be bleached by moistening the fabric and holding it under a sunlamp.

Grass stains: Soak stained area with liquid detergent; wash out with white vinegar.

Pet stains: Wash with white vinegar; rub with wet towel.

Bloodstains: A cool saltwater solution will remove blood stains from clothing. For stubborn blood spots apply ammonia before washing.

Leather gloves: Use lukewarm water and mild soap. Do not rinse completely. Soap left in gloves will help keep the leather soft.

Shoes: Coat the edges of the soles of new shoes with colorless nail polish. This helps retain finish and prevent scuffing. Cover scuff marks on black shoes with India ink and polish. Rub scuff marks on brown shoes with milk to which a few drops of ammonia have been added. When dry, polish with a soft cloth.

Ballpoint ink: Hair spray will remove ballpoint ink marks from clothing. There are a number of good spot removers and cleaning agents on the market. Be sure to follow exactly the directions on the can or bottle.

Warning: Do not mix cleaning agents. They are chemicals and may combine with disastrous results. Ammonia and chlorine cleansers or bowl cleaners (for toilets), for example, give off poisonous fumes.

BARGAINS IN THE SUPERMARKET

There are many bargains in food, but you must look for them when you shop. You aren't saving anything if the canned or frozen vegetables you get for a few pennies less than the standard brands are of such poor quality you won't eat them. When you find a good brand name, remember it and look for it again. Packers are usually consistent in quality, whether good or only fair. Note the weight of the contents marked on the can or package. Your eye might not see the

If you want favor with both God and man, and a reputation for good judgment and common sense, then trust the Lord completely; don't ever trust yourself.
PROVERBS 3:4, 5

To prevent flower vases from leaving white stains on table tops, either set the vase on a coaster, or melt paraffin and coat the inside of the vase with wax before filling with water. Be sure to twirl the vase around so that it is thoroughly coated.

He grants good sense to the godly. . . .
PROVERBS 2:7

difference of an ounce or two, but the net weight will point out which brand gives you the most value for your money.

Many generic foods cost less than well advertised "name" products and, in many cases, are just as good. That is particularly true of paper products. In addition, canned fruits and vegetables and soda crackers may be just as tasty and can be a real bargain. We would suggest that you limit your purchases of generic items to one of a kind until you are sure that you are satisfied with them.

By shopping wisely you can make substantial savings on your food budget and make your husband think you are the smartest woman in the world. Write out a grocery list so you don't succumb to the temptation of "impulse buying." Check your list against the newspaper ads to take advantage of the savings offered on the specials.

Don't forget the many prepared foods when you are shopping. Prepackaged macaroni and cheese dinners, for example, offer a considerable saving in time and money over preparing macaroni and cheese yourself. This is true of many cake and cookie mixes, pizza, chow mein, and other convenience foods.

It is often difficult to shop wisely. The advertising clamor is so noisy and the claims so extravagant that it is difficult to know whom to believe and what to buy. It is seldom wise to buy the cheapest product. In the case of detergents (and many other things) you will usually have to use twice or three times as much of a cheap brand as you will of a better one.

Check the weight on the package of a brand of like quality and compare prices. When choosing a store (many careful women go where the specials are the most attractive, even though it means going to a different store each week) be guided only by the prices and not by what the store is giving away.

When buying plastic wrap, aluminum foil, paper towels, or bathroom tissue, check the length and make sure you are getting the best price per foot.

Regardless of where you shop, you will occasionally get milk that has soured or meat or vegetables or fruit that aren't what they should be. Don't be afraid to return those items; most store managers want you to do so.

Choose fresh produce carefully to get the most for your money. You may find a real buy on overripe bananas, for example, but if you haven't time to make a banana cake or bread it is better to leave them at the store. Nothing is a bargain, regardless of price, unless you need it.

Riches can disappear fast. And the king's crown doesn't stay in his family forever—so watch your business interests closely. Know the state of your flocks and your herds; then there will be lamb's wool enough for clothing, and goat's milk enough for food for all your household after the hay is harvested, and the new crop appears, and the mountain grasses are gathered in.
PROVERBS
27:23-27

Beans: String beans are expensive no matter what the price if the pods are bulging and whitish in color.

Broccoli with open buds that have yellow or purple blossoms is also a bad buy.

Cabbage: Be sure to check the weight. It should be heavy for its size and have no yellow leaves. If there is decay or worm damage at the core, it's better to pass it up.

Carrots should be firm, bright in color, and have no green around the top.

Cauliflower must be white, clean, and have no specks. If the head is dirty or has black spots, it is not for you.

Celery stalks may be white or green depending on the variety, but they should be solid and free from blemishes.

Sweet corn is best when eaten within a few hours of the time it has been picked. However, that is possible only in areas where it is grown. Examine sweet corn with care. Be sure the kernels are plump and milky. Very small kernels indicate immaturity. You not only get little for your money, but there is little flavor in what you do get. Large, hard kernels are too mature and no more flavorful than the small ones.

Cucumbers that are dull and yellow in color are not desirable.

Eggplant should be dark and glossy, not wilted or spongy.

Grapefruit should be chosen with care. The heavier grapefruit are the juiciest. Surface blemishes might make the grapefruit look inferior to those that are clear, but they do not affect the quality.

Lettuce: When buying head lettuce select one that is heavy and firm. It should be dark green and crisp. If you find rust streaks or spots on the inside, take it back.

Onions: Check to be sure there are no soft, dark spots which indicate spoilage.

Oranges: Buy oranges the same way you do grapefruit. Usually small oranges are the most economical, but they should be firm and have no decayed spots. Learn whether an orange is heavy or light by weighing it in your hand. Thin-skinned oranges give more value for your money.

Peppers should be thick-skinned and dark green in color. They should be well shaped. Avoid those with dark spots.

Potatoes should be free from blemishes, reasonably clean, and not shriveled. They should not have green spots beneath the skin as this may cause a bitter flavor. White potatoes are usually best for baking.

Tomatoes should be solid and glossy and heavy for their size.

A constant dripping on a rainy day and a cranky woman are much alike.
PROVERBS 27:15

Why spend your money on foodstuffs that don't give you strength? Why pay for groceries that don't do you any good? Listen and I'll tell you where to get food to fatten up your soul!
ISAIAH 55:2

REFRIGERATION GUIDE

Freeze leftover whipping cream in dabs on wax paper and store in tightly covered container. Use it for topping on desserts.

Deep colors such as red, blue, green, black, and bright yellow should never be put into the wash with other clothes the first time they are washed. Wash separately until you are sure they are fadeproof.

Perishable Food	Preparation and Care	Length of Refrigeration
DAIRY PRODUCTS		
Cream and milk	Wipe off container, refrigerate immediately.	3 to 4 days
Buttermilk	Same as above.	Use in 2 or 3 days
Sour cream	Same as above.	Use in 2 or 3 days
Butter and margarine	Store 1 to 2 days' supply in butter-keeper; keep remainder wrapped in store container.	1 to 2 weeks; wrapped will keep for several months
Natural cheese	Keep wrapped, store on any shelf of refrigerator. Once opened, rewrap with plastic wrap or foil.	2 to 3 weeks
Hard cheese	Treat as above; when stored for long periods, dip cut surface in hot paraffin.	May be stored 3 to 4 months, though may become strong
Soft cheese, as cottage cheese, cream cheese, limburger, etc.	Cheese with strong aroma should be kept tightly wrapped and in air-tight glass or plastic containers.	Should be used in 4 to 5 days
Eggs	Store in egg rack or keep in container.	About 2 weeks; use cracked eggs immediately
FRUITS		
Grapefruit Oranges Lemons Limes	Store in crisper box.	1 week
Apples Apricots Grapes Peaches Pears Plums	Wash, allow to ripen at room temperature; store in crisper when ripe.	Use within 1 week
Avocados Bananas	Purchase only supply needed for short time.	Use in 2 to 3 days
Melons	Wrap in foil or plastic	Use within 5 to 7 days

Perishable Food	Preparation and Care	Length of Refrigeration
Mangoes Pineapple	wrap after cutting as odor permeates everything in refrigerator.	
Strawberries Raspberries Cherries Other small fruit	Sort out soft fruit, replace in open woven basket or shallow pan in refrigerator; wash just before use; sugar just before serving.	Within 2 to 3 days
Opened canned fruit or juices	Put into plastic or glass-covered refrigerator dish.	Use in 2 to 3 days
FISH, POULTRY, MEATS		
Packaged fresh meats	If used promptly, leave in wrapper.	1 to 2 days
	If not, loosen wrapper at both ends, or rewrap loosely in foil or plastic wrap. Store in meat section.	3 to 4 days
	If you shop once a week, freeze meat you plan to use last.	Should be used within a week or two
Bulk fresh meat, as steak, veal, liver, pork chops, etc.	Open, store loosely wrapped in foil or waxed paper. Place in meat compartment.	2 to 3 days
Roasts	As fresh meat.	3 to 5 days
Ground meat	As fresh meat.	1 day
Bacon and ham	Keep in original packaging.	5 to 7 days
Wieners Sliced cold cuts	Keep in original packaging.	3 to 5 days
Unsliced cold bologna and sausage	Keep in original packaging.	3 to 6 days
Canned ham	Keep in original packaging.	See directions on can
Chicken Turkey Duck	Place in pan, cover loosely with wax paper or foil. If frozen, keep	Use within 2 days

For everything God made is good, and we may eat it if we are thankful for it.
1 TIMOTHY 4:4

A large empty detergent box makes a handy laundry room wastebasket. It is easily disposed of when full.

Even honey seems tasteless to a man who is full; but if he is hungry, he'll eat anything.
PROVERBS 27:7

Perishable Food	Preparation and Care	Length of Refrigeration
Goose	frozen until night before use, then set out in room.	
Fish	Loosen package or store in loosely covered dish.	Use within 2 days
All frozen meats	Keep frozen until day before you plan to use. Place on refrigerator shelf to thaw.	Treat as fresh
VEGETABLES (FRESH) Asparagus Broccoli Brussels sprouts	Open package and wash in cold water. Check and cut away bruised or bad spots. Drain slightly, store in crisper or closed plastic bag.	3 to 5 days
Cabbage Cauliflower Celery	Same as above.	Up to 1 week
Beets Carrots Radishes Green onions	Remove tops and roots, wash and drain. Place in plastic bag or air tight container.	1 week or more
Corn on the cob	If in shuck, leave until ready to prepare. If peeled, wash and store.	4 to 5 days
Leaf lettuce Spinach	Sort over for dirt or insects. Wash thoroughly and store, with a bit of moisture, in plastic bag.	2 to 4 days
Green peppers Cucumbers Tomatoes	Wash, dry, and store in crisper.	2 to 4 days
Fresh mushrooms	Sort, wash, and place loosely in shallow dish.	Use within 1 or 2 days as they darken rapidly
Potatoes Dry onions Eggplant Turnips Squash	These do not require refrigeration. Buy only as many as needed for 2 to 3 weeks.	

WEIGHTS AND MEASURES

3 teaspoons = 1 tablespoon
4 tablespoons = ¼ cup
5⅓ tablespoons = ⅓ cup
8 tablespoons = ½ cup
12 tablespoons = ¾ cup
16 tablespoons = 1 cup
2 tablespoons = 1 liquid ounce

1 cup = ½ pint
2 cups = 1 pint
4 cups = 1 quart
4 quarts = 1 gallon
8 quarts = 1 peck
4 pecks = 1 bushel

2 tablespoons butter = 1 ounce
½ cup butter = ¼ pound or 1 stick
1 cup butter = ½ pound or 2 sticks
2¼ cups white sugar = 1 pound
2¼ cups firmly packed brown sugar = 1 pound
3½ cups powdered sugar = 1 pound
4 cups sifted flour = 1 pound
1 tablespoon cornstarch = 2 tablespoons flour
2⅛ cups uncooked rice = 1 pound
1 square chocolate = 1 ounce
3 tablespoons cocoa + 1 tablespoon butter = 1 square chocolate
2 cups tiny marshmallows = ¼ pound
16 large marshmallows = ¼ pound
1 cup chopped nuts = ¼ pound
4 cups shredded American cheese = 1 pound
6⅔ tablespoons cream cheese = 1 3-ounce package
7 coarsely crumbled salted crackers = 1 cup
9 finely rolled crackers = 1 cup
11 finely rolled graham crackers = 1 cup
½ cup evaporated milk + ½ cup water = 1 cup milk
1 lemon = 2½ to 3 tablespoons juice
12 to 14 egg yolks = 1 cup
8 to 10 egg whites = 1 cup
1⅓ tablespoons vinegar or 1½ tablespoons lemon juice + sweet
   milk to make 1 cup = 1 cup sour milk

Determination to be wise is the first step toward becoming wise!
PROVERBS 4:7

When measuring, spoon flour directly into measuring cup until it is heaped up; level with edge of spatula or straight knife. Dipping into the container with the measuring cup packs the flour. Sifting directly into the cup gives about one tablespoon under measure.

Brown sugar should be packed firmly enough to retain the shape of the cup when turned out.

ABBREVIATIONS

teasp. or tsp. = teaspoon
tbsp. = tablespoon
c. = cup
oz. = ounce
pt. = pint
qt. = quart
gal. = gallon
pk. = peck
bu. = bushel
lb. = pound

OVEN TEMPERATURES

250°-275°—very slow
300°-325°—slow
350°-375°—moderate
400°-425°—hot
450°-475°—very hot
500°-525°—extremely hot or broil

HINTS FOR MEASURING

To measure liquids—Put glass measuring cup on flat surface at eye level to read exact amount in cup.

To measure dry ingredients—Fill measuring cup to overflowing, then level off with the straight edge of knife. However, brown sugar must be tightly packed.

To measure shortening—Pack warm shortening tightly so no air holes are in measuring cup. Or for ½ cup shortening, fill cup ½ full of *cold* water, add shortening to 1 cup mark, then pour off water.

Entertaining Friends

USING YOUR HOME FOR CHRIST

An open door, a warm smile, and a gracious manner can be a vital Christian service for you and your husband and enlarge your friendships. The next time you go to Sunday school or church, look around. The shy couple on the back row may be hungry for Christian fellowship. Or they may be fumbling for spiritual guidance that will bring stability or the light of salvation to their lives.

Make the first move toward getting to know the people who are new to the church or those among your neighbors or acquaintances who seem to need friends. Ask them over for coffee after the evening service or, if you're very brave, for dinner. The conversation might be a bit strained until you get better acquainted, but you will be surprised at the way people will respond. You will have the joy of seeing people challenged by Christ through your friendliness and availability—if you are willing to work at it.

MENU IDEAS FOR ENTERTAINING

Even if you lived on your own before marriage, most of your entertaining was probably casual. Now that you're married, you will still entertain this way, but you will probably want to add the more formal sit-down dinner to your repertoire.

I'll never forget the first time I had my husband's parents over for dinner, or the first time our daughter Bonnie invited her in-laws for a meal. She asked them in a moment of rash courage and died a little at a time whenever she thought of it. She didn't think she could live through it, but she did. The meal was a great success and she found that this type of entertaining could be fun when she was properly prepared.

She wisely chose a menu she had already tried on her husband and prepared as much of the meal as possible the day before. She was afraid the last minute rush would give her the jitters and spoil the impression she wanted to make on Doug's father and mother as a composed, gracious hostess.

FOUR

Dear friends, let us practice loving each other, for love comes from God and those who are loving and kind show that they are children of God, and that they are getting to know him better.
1 JOHN 4:7

Honor goes to kind and gracious women. . . .
PROVERBS 11:16

Before guests come for dinner write your menu on a card and check it just before you sit down to eat. Many an experienced hostess has found her Jell-O salad in the refrigerator after the guests have gone home!

You might prefer another menu, but if not, this one should work for you.

Menu
Baked ham—buy either half a ham or have one sliced, ready to heat in foil. Wrap tightly to preserve the rich flavor.
Twice-baked potatoes* (prepared the day before)
Broccoli-cauliflower salad* (prepared the day before)
Frozen peas, creamed*
Hot rolls, butter, and marmalade
Filled angel food cake* (prepared the day before and refrigerated)
Hot tea or coffee

Or, you might be very brave and try a more challenging menu.

Menu
Rump roast (see meat chart)
Mashed potatoes*
Gravy*
Green bean casserole*
Tossed salad with your own french dressing*
French rolls* and butter
Pecan pie topped with whipped cream*
Coffee or tea

You undoubtedly learned as a teenager how to manage the details of entertaining at dinner by helping your mother, but having the full responsibility can be frustrating at first. However, it need not be. With proper planning you can invite guests in and be confident that everything will go well. Plan everything well in advance, allowing plenty of time to take care of any last minute problems that may arise. Set the table early and work out the seating arrangements before your guests arrive. A checklist will help you in your planning.

In the scurry of planning and preparation don't forget that the key to a pleasant evening is the gracious attitude of the host and hostess.

SETTING THE TABLE
For some reason food seems to taste better when it is attractively served in clean, lovely surroundings. It is easy to set a beautiful table if you remember a few basic rules.

Use one of the lovely tablecloths you got as wedding gifts. It doesn't matter whether it is linen, rayon, or cotton. All three lend themselves admirably to an informal dinner.

*Recipe in Part 2.

A woman named Martha welcomed them into her home. Her sister Mary sat on the floor, listening to Jesus as he talked. But Martha was the jittery type, and was worrying over the big dinner she was preparing. She came to Jesus and said, "Sir, doesn't it seem unfair to you that my sister just sits here while I do all the work? Tell her to come and help me."

But the Lord said to her, "Martha, dear friend, you are so upset over all these details! There is really only one thing worth being concerned about. Mary has discovered it—and I won't take it away from her."
LUKE 10:38-42

In setting the table allow at least eighteen inches between place settings, if possible. Your guests will be more comfortable if they have a little elbow room, and it will be easier for you to serve them.

The silver should be one inch from the edge of the table. Knives and spoons belong at the right side of the plate, the forks at the left.

The napkin, folded so the open corner is nearest the plate, is placed to the left of the fork or in the center of the plate. Water glasses should be placed at the point of the knife.

SEATING AND SERVING GUESTS

Custom dictates a certain formality in the seating of guests. Even when entertaining your family or one or two guests, authorities on such matters say that the host and hostess should sit at opposite ends of the table. For obvious reasons I usually choose the place at the end of the table nearest the kitchen.

The guest of honor, if a man, should be seated at your right. The lady guest of honor should sit to the right of your husband. Other guests fill in the remaining places at the table.

Guests should be served from the left when serving dishes are passed. Beverages, however, are served from the right and additional silver, if it is needed, is placed from the right.

Plates are removed from the left, and all the dishes from one guest's place should be removed before going to the next. Water glasses are filled three-fourths full, from the right, and without removing the glass from the table. The dessert is served from the left.

BUFFET ENTERTAINING

Buffet entertaining is an easy, imaginative way to entertain. It is a nice way to entertain after church on Sunday night, or any time you want to have some friends in. You can invite more people and not worry so much about seating around a table. Just be sure to have sturdy plates and an occasional table or two to accommodate a glass of water or a cup of coffee should the need arise.

If you choose this method you might want to serve fruit or vegetable juice in the living room before the guests enter the dining area. Then you will be free to add last-minute touches to the buffet table.

If you are serving hot foods, you might find it best to serve the guests those dishes yourself in order to speed up the serving. Guests at a buffet should be able to eat everything without using a knife.

Setting a buffet table is simple. You will need napkins, plates, and silverware, one or two hot dishes, a cold dish, a tossed salad, buttered rolls, and relishes. The silver should be placed at the end of the

Ability to give wise advice satisfies like a good meal!
PROVERBS 18:20

Use a little spray starch on your new cotton dress before each wearing and you will have that "freshly new" look.

If you can find a truly good wife, she is worth more than precious gems!
PROVERBS 31:10

table where it can be picked up last.

Dessert may be served from the buffet table, which has been cleared after your guests have eaten all they wish. However, you may want to arrange dessert servings in the kitchen and pass them individually.

You can set up the table beforehand and have much of your food prepared and in the refrigerator, ready to set out just before serving time.

Only fools refuse to be taught.
PROVERBS 1:8

I love finger foods, so perhaps that is the reason for my love of buffets. These are some of the things I like to serve and they have been the most rewarding.

In everything you do, put God first, and he will direct you and crown your efforts with success.
PROVERBS 3:6

Menu
Clam dip*—served with potato chips
Hot chili dip*—served with corn chips
Impossible Quiche* (one of these for every six people)
Carrot cake*
Ribbon sandwiches*
A tray of veggies (cauliflower, olives, carrot sticks, celery sticks, radishes, green onions, and marinated artichokes)
Cocktail puffs*
Ham roll-ups*
Coffee
Tea
Punch or cider

Arrange the drinks and cups and glasses at one end of the table, along with cream, sugar, and artificial sweetener. Then set a colorful plate of veggies in the middle, in front of the candles, flowers, or whatever you use for a centerpiece. Arrange some pretty napkins in front of this. Then fill in on either side with the dips, chips in baskets, and the quiche and cocktail puffs. Add the ham roll-ups and the ribbon sandwiches. Leave the desserts whole, or serve individual servings on small plates if you have the room. Or put the desserts on another table, or even in another room.

UNEXPECTED GUESTS
Perhaps you are dreading the time guests will drop in unexpectedly. I used to tremble at the thought. When I was first married a knock at the door a few minutes before mealtime was enough to plunge me into a migraine. Then I learned a secret from an older, more experi-

*Recipe in Part 2.

enced friend who was a marvel to those who knew her for the way she was able to prepare for guests on short notice.

"I'd be as panicked as anyone if I had to prepare for guests when I didn't have anything on hand and the stores were closed," she assured me.

But she wasn't upset because she kept food on hand for unannounced guests. I followed her example and was never flustered by unexpected company.

My Emergency Rations
Instant mashed potatoes
Small box of dried milk
Tin or two of canned meat, ham, Vienna sausages, or tuna
Can of baked beans (Baked beans topped with Vienna sausages have saved my life more times than I can count!)
Box or two of fancy crackers
Cake mix
Canned pie filling (blueberry is my choice) to top the cake
Can of fruit cocktail (You can leave this in the freezer for weeks; remove both ends of can, slide out fruit, slice thick or thin, depending upon how many slices you need, put on salad plate, top with a dab of mayonnaise.)

For very little money, you can be prepared for any emergency. Like my friend, you will no longer dread having guests drop in at mealtime, and you will become known as the perfect hostess.

The man who finds a wife finds a good thing; she is a blessing to him from the Lord.
PROVERBS 18:22

Never forget to be truthful and kind. Hold these virtues tightly. Write them deep within your heart.
PROVERBS 3:3

Planning Menus

FIVE

BREAKFAST MENUS

You can put a bowl of cold cereal and a lukewarm cup of coffee before your husband in the morning and he may not mind for a while. But if you want to send him to work with a bounce in his step, you will do better than that.

These menus should be only a starting place. A little thought and ingenuity can give you endless variety.

Let me see your kindness in the morning, for I am trusting you. . . .
PSALM 143:8

Stewed prunes*
Scrambled eggs*
Whole-wheat toast
Butter
Beverage

Apricot nectar
Sausages*
Coffee cake* *(see recipe for rich roll dough)*
Beverage

Tomato juice
Bacon*
French toast*
Syrup*
Beverage

Grapefruit ice*
Hot rolls*
Butter
Beverage

Broiled grapefruit half*
Cold cereal and milk
Canadian bacon*
Panfried eggs*
Beverage

Berries and cream *(see section on fresh fruits)*
Soft-boiled eggs*
Whole-wheat toast
Butter
Beverage

Commit your work to the Lord, then it will succeed.
PROVERBS 16:3

Cold cereal with bananas and milk
Scrambled eggs with chipped beef*
Toast
Butter
Jelly
Beverage

Peaches, sliced and sugared
Bacon*
Waffles*
Syrup*
Butter
Beverage

Melon wedge *(see fruit section)*
Ham*
Biscuits* *(use our recipe or a mix)*
Butter
Honey
Beverage

Grape juice
Cold cereal
Bran muffins*
Jelly
Butter
Beverage

Tomato juice
Sausage ring*
Blueberry muffins*
Jelly
Butter
Beverage

Grapefruit half
Griddle cakes* *(or use mix)*
Butter
Syrup*
Broiled bacon*
Beverage

*Recipe in Part 2.

Baked apples* *(baked the night before)*
Bacon and egg cups*
Hot rolls* *(or buy at the bakery)*
Butter
Jelly
Beverage

Chilled fruit cocktail
Pancakes*
Maple syrup*
Sausages*
Butter
Beverage

Grapefruit juice
Poached egg on toast*
Hot cereal and milk
Butter
Beverage

This is the day the Lord has made. We will rejoice and be glad in it.
PSALM 118:24

LUNCH MENUS

If you and your husband both work, fixing lunch will be the making of a few sandwiches and filling a thermos with tea or coffee. But you may be one who has to prepare a meal at noon. These menus have been chosen with a hurried noon hour in mind.

Italian spaghetti*
Garlic bread*
Butter
Tossed salad*
Apple-pear pie*
Beverage

Oyster stew* (in season)
Crackers
Celery sticks
Radishes and pickles
Cake
Beverage

Chili con carne*
Celery sticks
Crackers
Butter
Baked apples*
Beverage

Line kitchen drawers with adhesive plastic linings and they'll wipe clean easily. This works fine in cosmetic drawers also.

Hot beef sandwiches (warmed-over gravy, sliced roast beef served on toast)
Pineapple ring on cottage cheese
Ice cream
Beverage

Chef's salad*
Crackers, garlic sticks, etc.
Canned fruit
Cookies
Beverage

Scalloped potatoes and Spam*
Tossed salad*
Bread or rolls
Butter
Cookies
Beverage

Lunch meats and cheeses
Bread or rolls
Butter
Potato chips and dip
Apple crisp*
Beverage

Frank boats*
Potato chips
Canned pears
Cookies
Beverage

Potato soup*
Cold meat sandwiches
Celery and carrot sticks
Instant chocolate pudding
Beverage

Grilled cheese sandwiches*
Cream of tomato soup (canned)
Lettuce wedge with dressing
Beverage

Creamed dried beef on toast*
Banana salad*
Sherbet
Beverage

Red kidney bean salad*
Toast
Butter
Fresh fruit
Beverage

*Recipe in Part 2.

Broiled franks wrapped
   in bacon*
Potato salad*
Pineapple-cheese
   ringaround*
Bread or rolls
Butter
Beverage

Hamburgers
Potato chips
Ice cream
Beverage

Ham sandwiches
Fritos
Fruit parfait*
Beverage

Macaroni-tuna salad*
Toast
Butter
Jelly
Chopped apple salad*
Beverage

*A cheerful heart
does good like medi-
cine. . . .*
PROVERBS 17:22

DINNER MENUS

The evening meal will require your special attention and care. Dinner time should be one of the high points of the day. There is time to linger at the table in the evening—time for you and your husband to get acquainted again after a day apart. Little frills that add so much to the enjoyment of a meal should be considered—an especially attractive table, your husband's favorite dish, or the dessert he likes the best. He will appreciate the little extra touches just as you appreciate his consideration and kindness.

And so the dinner menus we have included are more elaborate than those suggested for breakfast and lunch. You may not be able to prepare a large meal every night, but it is wise to do so as often as possible.

*Put wet garbage in
empty milk cartons
to keep the garbage
pail clean and dry.*

Fried chicken*
Mashed potatoes*
Gravy*
Buttered corn*
Tossed salad*
Corn muffins*
Butter
Apple pie*
Sharp cheese wedge
Beverage

Fried halibut*
Parsleyed potatoes*
Buttered frozen peas*
Tomato wedge on lettuce
Hot dilly bread*
Butter
Pecan pie* with
   whipped cream
Beverage

Roast beef*
Butter-crumbed potatoes*
Creamed peas*
Orange-cream Jell-O salad*
Parkerhouse rolls
Date chocolate chip cake*
Whipped cream*
Beverage

Spaghetti*
Parmesan cheese
Celery and lettuce
   wedges
Strawberry shortcake*
Beverage

Salmon supper*
Lettuce wedge with
   french dressing*
Strawberry parfait*
Beverage

Cordon Bleu*
Potato salad*
Baked green bean cas-
   serole*
Fresh fruit and cheese
   plate

*Recipe in Part 2.

Any enterprise is built by wise planning. . . .
PROVERBS 24:3

Individual meat loaves*
Quick scalloped potatoes*
Green bean casserole*
Coleslaw* and carrot sticks
Biscuits* and butter
Banana cake*
Beverage

Pork steak supreme*
Scalloped shredded potatoes
Cauliflower with cheese sauce*
Rye bread
Apple cake* with ice cream
Beverage

Baked ham* with raisin sauce*
Twice-baked potatoes* *(prepare the day before)*
Candied squash*
Pineapple-cheese ring-around*
Hot rolls
Gingerbread with whipped cream*
Beverage

Roast chicken* and dressing*
Mashed potatoes* and gravy*
Harvard beets*
Sunburst salad*
Tea rolls
Chocolate cream pie*
Beverage

Liver and onions*
Mashed potatoes*
Onion gravy*
Buttered carrots
Fruit plate*
Bran muffins*
Surprise peach pudding*
Beverage

Broiled steak*
French fried potatoes* *(buy them frozen if you like)*
Tossed salad*
Pineapple delight*
Beverage

Don't leave grease or fat in a pan on the stove unattended; it may ignite into a serious fire quickly.

Plug the electrical cord into the appliance first *and then into the wall outlet, just as a safety precaution.*

Stuffed pork chops*
Baked potatoes* and butter
Buttered broccoli*
Fruit salad*
Sherbet
Beverage

Barb's Chicken Divan*
Buttered carrots
Cottage cheese salad*
Bran muffins*
Pineapple cake*

Beef brisket*
Baked potatoes*
Spinach casserole*
Hot rolls*
Norma's Strawberry Cake*

Magnificent chicken*
Creamed macaroni*
Green salad
Chocolate torte dessert*

Pat's Beef Stew*
Hard rolls
Banana bundt cake*

Baked stew*
Relishes
Pineapple upside-down cake*
Beverage

Tuna-egg casserole*
Pat's Salad*
Chocolate pie supreme*

*Recipe in Part 2.

MEALS IN A MINUTE

Have you ever seen your mother rush home from a meeting, whip into the kitchen, and a few minutes later call the family to a tasty, attractive dinner? It isn't magic; it just seems that way. With proper planning and a little practice, you too can rush a well-balanced meal to the table.

Menu
Goulash*
Lettuce wedge and your favorite dressing
Whipped gelatin freeze*
Beverage

Menu
Skillet dinner*
Celery sticks
Apple and cheese wedges*
Coffee or tea

There are four things that are small, but un-usually wise: Ants: they aren't strong, but store up food for the winter. . . .
PROVERBS
30:24, 25

*Recipe in Part 2.

RECIPES

PART

2

Appetizers and Snacks

APPETIZERS

VERNA'S CHEESE SPREAD

Grind coarsely 10-ounce package medium sharp cheese, ½ jar sweet pickles, 1 small can pimiento; add 2 teaspoons pickle juice.

Mix with ½ teaspoon onion salt and enough mayonnaise to make it easy to spread. Delicious on crackers or dainty open-faced sandwiches.

CHEESE-OLIVE STUFFED DILLS

Hollow out large whole dill pickle; fill loosely with cheese spread. Force pimiento stuffed olives into cavity, using just enough olives to fill cavity. Chill and slice.

TOMATO HORS D'OEUVRES

Cut firm tomatoes into ½-inch wedges; scoop out inside. Fill with cream cheese mixed with anchovy paste; garnish with strips of ripe olives.

MEAT HORS D'OEUVRES

Cut cooked turkey or chicken in strips about 2 inches long and ½-inch wide; roll and secure with toothpick. Dip one end in mayonnaise mixed with a little catsup; roll dipped end in chopped pistachio nuts.

CHEESE TIDBITS

Cut sharp cheese into ½-inch squares; wrap each square in a narrow strip of boiled ham; fasten with toothpick.

BLUE CHEESE CELERY BITS

Press blue cheese through sieve; add cream to make a smooth paste. Fill green celery stalks using pastry tube or fork; sprinkle with paprika; chill until firm. Cut into bite-sized pieces.

APPLE AND CHEESE WEDGES

Quarter and core one or two apples. Top each wedge with cream cheese and chopped nuts.

COCKTAIL PUFFS

1 cup water
½ cup margarine
1 cup flour
4 eggs

In a 2-quart saucepan, bring water and butter to a boil, boiling until butter melts. Remove from heat and stir in flour. Beat until the mixture forms a ball. Then stir in the eggs one at a time until blended. Spoon by teaspoonfuls onto a greased cookie sheet. Bake at 400° 25 minutes. Fill with cream filling or with chicken or tuna salad.

HOT CHILI DIP

1 pound Velveeta cheese
1 16-ounce can chili
   without beans
1 4-ounce can chopped
   green chilis
5 green onions, chopped

Combine all ingredients and let simmer on low temperature for 2 or 3 hours. A slow cooker set on low is an excellent way to prepare this dip. Serve with corn chips in a pot that will stay hot.

LOUISE'S CLAM DIP

2 cups whipping cream
3 ounces cream cheese
2 4-ounce cans clams

Whip cream until very stiff. Soften cheese and gently mix with cream. Add clams and mix. Save liquid from clams to thin dip if it becomes too stiff. Serve with your favorite snack crackers.

CHEESE BALL

8 ounces cream cheese
3 ounces blue cheese
¼ cup dried, chopped
   parsley
1 tablespoon onion
½ cup chopped pecans

Soften cream cheese, crumble blue cheese, and mix with your hands. Work in the parsley and finely chopped onion. Make a ball. Roll in chopped pecans. Decorate with stuffed green olives if desired. Chill and serve with snack crackers.

GUACAMOLE

2 or 3 ripe avocados
   (mashed)
Add:
3 tablespoons diced
   onions
1 teaspoon lime juice
1 diced tomato
Garlic salt to taste

Mix all ingredients well.

DILL DIP

½ cup sour cream
½ cup mayonnaise
2 tablespoons dill weed
Dash of Beaumonde
   seasoning

Mix all ingredients well and chill.

CHEESE DIP

4 small packages cream
   cheese
1 carton old-fashioned
   cottage cheese, mashed
1 bottle catsup
1 package dry onion
   soup mix
1 cup half and half
½ cup sugar

Mix all ingredients well, chill and serve.

SNACKS

CHOCOLATE DELIGHTS (TING-A-LINGS)

Melt chocolate chips in pan over hot water. Cool to room temperature. Stir cereal into chocolate until thoroughly coated; spoon onto waxed paper. Place in refrigerator until hardened, 2 to 3 hours.

4 cups Wheaties
1 6-ounce package chocolate chips

POPCORN BALLS

Combine sugar, water, vinegar, syrup, and salt; stir until sugar dissolves. Cook to hard ball stage (256° on candy thermometer). Add vanilla and cook to light-crack stage. Remove from heat; add butter and food coloring. Pour slowly over popcorn, mixing thoroughly. Spread butter or margarine on hands and press popcorn into balls. This is fun to do with two working together, so get your husband into the act.

1 cup sugar
½ cup water
1 teaspoon vinegar
2 tablespoons light corn syrup
½ teaspoon salt
1 tablespoon butter
½ teaspoon red food coloring
6 cups popped corn

EASY CARAMEL CORN

Combine caramels and water in top of double boiler and set over simmering water. Heat until caramels are melted, stirring occasionally. Combine popped corn and peanuts in large buttered bowl. Pour caramel mixture over corn and toss with two buttered wooden spoons until corn and nuts are well coated. Spread in single layer on greased cookie sheet. Separate into bite-sized pieces when cool.

30 vanilla caramels (about ½ pound)
2 tablespoons water
5 cups popped corn
1 cup salted peanuts

ICE CREAM FLOATS

Place 2 or 3 generous scoops of ice cream (vanilla) in a large glass. Fill with any soft drink. Refreshing!

CINNAMON TOAST

Butter a slice of bread. Sprinkle liberally with sugar, then with cinnamon. Place under broiler in oven until toast is light brown. Cut in half and serve warm. Good with hot chocolate.

TV SNACK

Place dry ingredients in shallow pan. Melt butter, add sauce and seasonings. Pour over dry ingredients and mix thoroughly. Bake in 225° oven 1 hour, stirring every 15 minutes. (Makes a very large bowlful.)

1 cup Cheerios
2 cups tiny cheese crackers
2 cups Kix
2 cups pretzel sticks
½ pound mixed nuts
¼ cup butter or margarine
½ teaspoon Worcestershire sauce
Dash garlic salt
Dash celery salt

EASY SNACK COOKIES

Using graham crackers or your favorite store-bought cookie, spread with powdered sugar icing—yummy!

51

BACON–CHILI SAUCE SANDWICH

Toast bread. Butter, then spread with peanut butter. Cover with chili sauce and uncooked bacon slices. Place 3 inches under broiler, and broil until bacon is brown. Serve hot.

JAN'S PEANUT BUTTER CANDY

1 cup firmly packed
   brown sugar
1 cup white sugar
1 cup sour cream
¼ teaspoon salt
1 tablespoon vanilla
1 cup creamy peanut
   butter

Stir brown sugar, white sugar, sour cream, and salt until well-blended. Cook over medium heat stirring occasionally until mixture reaches the soft ball stage (236°). Remove from heat and cool to lukewarm. Stir in vanilla and peanut butter. Pour into greased 9" x 13" pan. Cool. Cut and serve.

ONION RINGS

3 large onions
1 cup flour
½ cup cornstarch
1 teaspoon baking soda
½ teaspoon salt
1½ cups ice water

Slice onions and cover with ice water for two hours.

Combine flour, cornstarch, baking soda, and salt. Add 1½ cups ice water all at once and whisk until smooth. Refrigerate at least 1 hour before using.

Heat oil to 375°. Drain onions well. Dust with flour to be sure they are dry. Add onions to batter. Fry a few at a time for 3 or 4 minutes, turning once until crisp and brown. Drain and salt.

Beverages

SEVEN

COFFEE

When your grandmother was a girl, coffee came to the store in large burlap bags and was ground to the customer's specifications when it was purchased. Today you have an even wider range of grinds than she had. That makes it all the more important that you use the correct grind for your particular coffeepot. After you have opened a can of coffee be sure to store it in a tightly closed container. Prolonged exposure to air will steal the flavor from even the best brand.

There are ways of economizing, but it is seldom wise to select a cheap brand of coffee. Most housewives have a jar of instant coffee on hand. Good brands of instant coffee are almost as tasty as the regular variety and, on occasion, they are much handier.

Percolator coffee is made by placing measured, freshly drawn cold water into the coffeepot. Regular grind coffee is placed in the top compartment and covered. Use one tablespoonful of coffee for each measuring cup of water. Bring the water to the boiling point and when the brew begins to percolate, reduce heat. Continue percolating gently for five minutes.

Vacuum coffee makers operate by having fresh cold water in the lower bowl of the coffee maker and fine grind, or vacuum coffee, in the upper bowl. Place coffee maker on heat. When the water has come to the top of the coffee maker reduce heat or remove coffee maker from the burner. (Follow instructions that came with the coffee maker.) After coffee has returned to the lower part of the coffee maker, remove the upper part and serve coffee as soon as possible. Place over low heat to keep the coffee hot.

There are many brands of *automatic drip* coffee makers on the shelves today. They come with detailed directions and are very similar to one another.

Line the coffee holder basket with a paper coffee filter. Add recommended grind (one rounded teaspoon of coffee per cup). Place the holder in place and pour water into the reservoir. Plug in the coffee maker and turn to BREW. When the coffee stops dripping,

"If anyone is thirsty, let him come to me and drink."
JOHN 7:37b

To separate two glasses that are stuck together, fill the inside glass with cold water and set the outer glass in warm water. They will separate easily in a few minutes.

To remove fruit or coffee stains from a tablecloth, pour boiling water held about 12 inches above the cloth until the stain vanishes. Wash as usual.

turn the dial to WARM. You may wish to use a bit more coffee or a bit less to adjust the strength to your taste.

Many people today are excited about making *Melita* coffee. You can purchase a one-cup funnel-shaped *Melita* coffee maker with filters to fit, or a larger family-sized *Melita* coffee maker. The method is to use one slightly rounded teaspoon of finely ground coffee, usually drip grind. Place unit over a coffee cup and pour one cup of boiling water over the coffee. The larger maker would use one slightly rounded teaspoon coffee per cup of boiling water. It can be increased or decreased to make the coffee to your taste. Delicious!

TEA

Preheat the teapot with warm water before starting to make tea. Use one teaspoon tea for each cup of water. Put into teapot and add actively boiling water. Allow to steep three minutes (more for stronger tea) before serving. Remember, the water must be really boiling actively—just "hot" isn't good enough!

If you use tea bags allow one tea bag for two cups of tea and proceed as directed above. Remove the bags after the tea has steeped for three minutes.

Instant tea is excellent for either hot or iced tea. Follow the directions on the container.

Sun tea makes a tasty iced tea. Simply fill a gallon-size glass jar with cold water, add nine tea bags, cover, and set in the sun for three or four hours.

While instant tea makes excellent iced tea, the occasion may arise when you have to make it with tea bags or loose tea. Make the tea double strength using two teaspoons of tea or one tea bag for each cup of water. Put hot tea in a pitcher or enameled saucepan; cool. To serve, pour over ice in glasses and serve with lemon wedges and sugar. Iced tea has a tendency to become cloudy and strong if stored in the refrigerator.

LEMONADE

Be sure there are no seeds in lemon juice, but do not strain. Add sugar and ice to juice and stir until ice is almost dissolved, or add water to suit taste. Serve at once. About 6 servings.

HOT SPICED TOMATO JUICE

Combine ingredients and simmer ½ hour. Serve hot.

"But the water I give them," he said, "becomes a perpetual spring within them, watering them forever with eternal life."
JOHN 4:14

Store extra ice cubes in a plastic bag in the freezer.

½ cup freshly squeezed lemon juice
½ cup sugar to taste
20 large ice cubes

1 46-ounce can tomato juice
6 tablespoons brown sugar
6 whole cloves
2-2½ sticks cinnamon
½ lemon, sliced

VERNA'S FRUIT PUNCH

1 46-ounce can each Hawaiian punch, pineapple-grapefruit juice, orange-pineapple juice. Combine; add 2 bottles strawberry soda and 2 bottles 7-Up. Add ice and serve. Makes about 5 quarts.

APRICOT LIME DRINK
(Delicious as an appetizer.)
Pour chilled apricot nectar into small glasses; top with a small scoop of lime sherbet.

I reach out for you. I thirst for you as parched land thirsts for rain.
PSALM 143:6

HOT CHOCOLATE

Melt chocolate squares in hot water in top of double boiler; add sugar and salt. Cook over direct heat 4 minutes, stirring constantly. Add milk gradually and heat over low flame, stirring constantly. Serves 5.

2 1-ounce squares
   unsweetened
   chocolate
1 cup hot water
Dash of salt
3 to 4 tablespoons sugar
3 cups milk

BANANA PUNCH

Mix ingredients in blender and freeze. When ready to use, set it out and add 3 bottles of 7-Up. Stir and serve.

4 bananas
2 cups sugar
1 small can unsweetened
   pineapple juice
1 can frozen orange
   juice
3 cans water
1 cup concentrated
   lemon juice

JAN'S PROM PUNCH

Mix all ingredients well.

   Freeze one day or more. You can freeze all in one container or several if you're using it at different times. Add 3 large bottles of ginger ale as you serve.

2 46-ounce cans
   unsweetened
   pineapple juice
2 packages fruit-flavored
   drink crystals
1 cup sugar
1 12-ounce can frozen
   orange juice
   concentrate

Breads

EIGHT

QUICK BREADS

A "Bread of Life" or "Precious Promise Box" is available at any religious book or gift store. Why don't you get one and memorize a verse each day as you work? I keep mine by the kitchen sink where I see it many times each day. You will find that often God will give you a special verse, one that exactly meets your need at the moment.

After you have memorized a verse, go on to another, but remember to review the week's verses to implant God's Word firmly in your heart.

I have thought much about your words, and stored them in my heart so that they would hold me back from sin.
PSALM 119:11

BAKING POWDER BISCUITS

Sift dry ingredients and blend with shortening, using hands. (The warmth of your hands will help to soften the shortening to the right consistency.) Mixture should resemble crumbs the size of small peas. Slowly add milk until batter is stiff enough to handle easily. Turn out onto floured board or paper towel; fold or knead about 10 times.

Roll to ¾-inch thickness and cut with any round cutter. Place on greased cookie sheet or any shallow pan, lightly rerolling the remaining pieces of dough and cutting again until the dough is entirely used. Biscuits may either touch or be placed an inch apart.

Bake in hot oven (450°) 12 to 18 minutes.

2 cups flour
3 teaspoons baking
  powder
½ teaspoon salt
⅓ cup shortening
¾ to ⅞ cup milk

DATE NUT BREAD

Pour boiling water over cut up dates; add brown sugar and butter. Stir and let cool. Sift flour with salt and soda. Stir egg into cooled date mixture. Add dry ingredients and rum flavoring; beat well. Stir in nuts and turn into 1 large well-greased loaf pan or 2 small pans. Bake 1 hour and 10 minutes in moderate oven (350°).

Here is another opportunity to put something in the freezer for unexpected guests. You can eat your date bread and have it too!

1 6-ounce package dates
¾ cup boiling water
½ cup brown sugar,
  firmly packed
¼ cup butter or
  margarine
1¾ cups flour
¾ teaspoon salt
1 teaspoon baking soda
1 beaten egg
1½ teaspoons rum
  flavoring
½ cup chopped nuts

BISCUIT MIX

6 cups of flour
2½ tablespoons baking powder
1 tablespoon salt
1 cup shortening

This is nice to have on hand in a tightly covered container in your refrigerator. It keeps for several months if refrigerated. You can use any amount, adding enough milk to make dough the right consistency. This is another of the little tricks that permit you to perform magic in your kitchen. Proceed as in the baking powder biscuit recipe. Store in covered jar.

BANANA BREAD

½ cup shortening
1 cup sugar
2 eggs
3 or 4 very ripe bananas, mashed
2 cups flour
1 teaspoon baking soda
½ cup nuts

Cream shortening and sugar; add eggs and banana, then combined dry ingredients. Fold in nuts, and bake in two small or one large loaf pan. The pans should be one-half full. Bake 40 minutes at 350°. Note: It's nice to bake this in small pans. After they have cooled, wrap one tightly in foil or plastic and freeze. One loaf can be eaten and you'll have a nice fresh loaf in the freezer when you need it.

BRAN MUFFINS

1 cup 100% bran cereal
1 cup milk
3 tablespoons melted shortening
¼ cup sugar or honey
1 slightly beaten egg
1 cup flour
½ teaspoon salt
3 teaspoons baking powder

Combine milk and bran; let stand 10 minutes. Beat shortening with sugar until light; add egg and beat. Stir in bran mixture; add flour, baking powder, and salt. Grease muffin tins and fill one-half full. Bake (400°) 25 to 30 minutes. Makes 14 muffins.

CORN BREAD

1 cup yellow corn meal
1 cup flour
1 teaspoon salt
3½ teaspoons baking powder
2 tablespoons sugar
1 well-beaten egg
1 cup milk
¼ cup melted shortening

Sift together flour, salt, baking powder, and sugar; mix with corn meal. Combine egg, milk, and shortening. Add to dry ingredients and stir with fork just until moistened. Bake in greased 9-inch square pan at 425° for 40 minutes. Note: If there is corn bread left over, wrap tightly in foil and freeze. Use the foil as a container when you reheat the bread.

WAFFLES

2 cups flour
3 teaspoons baking powder
½ teaspoon salt
3 eggs, separated
3½ tablespoons sugar
1¾ cups milk
¼ cup melted shortening

Mix dry ingredients thoroughly. Add sugar to stiffly beaten egg whites and beat until mixture stands in soft peaks. Beat egg yolks; add milk and shortening; pour into flour mixture. Beat until smooth. Fold in egg whites. Using ½ cup batter for each waffle, bake in hot waffle iron. Serve with butter and hot syrup. Makes six 7-inch waffles.

Note: Leftover waffles may be wrapped and frozen. When needed, unwrap and heat in toaster.

PANCAKES

Combine ingredients and beat until moist. Heat griddle to 350° and grease lightly. Bake until top side of pancake is full of little holes, then turn and bake until golden. Turn only once. Serve with prepared syrup or your own maple syrup and butter, with ham or sausage if desired.

2 cups flour
5 teaspoons baking powder
½ teaspoon salt
2½ tablespoons sugar
2 beaten eggs
2 cups milk (or 1 cup evaporated milk and 1 cup water)
5 tablespoons melted shortening

GINGERBREAD

Pour water over shortening; add molasses, sugar, and egg. Add sifted dry ingredients; beat until smooth. Bake in greased and floured 8-inch square pan in moderate oven (350°) 35 minutes. Cook in pan. Cut into squares and serve with whipped cream.

½ cup hot water
½ cup shortening
½ cup light molasses
½ cup brown sugar
1 well-beaten egg
1½ cups flour
½ teaspoon baking powder
1 teaspoon baking soda
¾ teaspoon cinnamon
¾ teaspoon ginger
½ teaspoon salt

FRENCH TOAST

Mix ingredients. Dip bread (day old or fresh) into liquid mixture. Turn and dip other side. Fry in skilled or on griddle in a small amount of fat until brown. If you use butter or margarine, keep heat down to prevent burning. Serve with jelly, jam, or syrup.

1 cup milk
2 well-beaten eggs
½ teaspoon salt
Dash cinnamon or nutmeg, if desired

MAPLE SYRUP

Combine 1 cup sugar and ½ cup water. Stir until sugar is dissolved; bring to a boil. Add ½ teaspoon of maple flavoring. Serve hot on waffles or griddle cakes.

MILK TOAST

Pour ½ cup hot milk over slice of hot buttered toast. Serve immediately.

Jesus replied, "I am the Bread of Life. No one coming to me will ever be hungry again."
JOHN 6:35

MUFFINS

Sift dry ingredients; mix liquids thoroughly; add to dry ingredients. Stir until moist, but not smooth, as over-beating will make muffins tough. Fill well-greased muffin cups (or use paper cups) two-thirds full. Bake in hot oven (425°) 25 minutes. Makes 12.

1½ cups flour
4 teaspoons baking powder
½ teaspoon salt
1 tablespoon sugar
¾ cup milk
2 well-beaten eggs
¼ cup melted shortening

2 cups boiling water
2 cups 100% All Bran
1 cup margarine
3 cups white sugar
4 eggs
1 quart buttermilk
4 cups Kellogg's All Bran
1 teaspoon salt
5 teaspoons baking soda
5 cups flour

2 packages of yeast
¼ cup warm water
½ cup melted margarine
¾ cup milk
2 eggs, beaten
½ cup sugar
4 cups flour

Orange or lemon juice alone will not give a distinct flavor in baked goods but grated rind of either will.

BLUEBERRY MUFFINS

Use preceding recipe, but reduce milk to ½ cup and fold in ¾ cup fresh blueberries or 1 small can drained blueberries. Bake as above.

GARLIC BREAD

Cut unsliced loaf almost through into thick slices. Spread with melted butter seasoned with garlic salt or diced clove of garlic. Wrap bread in foil or paper bag and heat in oven about 10 minutes.

PAT'S BRAN MUFFINS

Pour boiling water over 100% All Bran in a small bowl. Cream margarine and sugar. Add eggs and beat with buttermilk and then add Kellogg's All Bran. Add dry ingredients and mix. Then fold in soaked bran. Bake in greased muffin tins at 400° for 15 to 20 minutes. This batter can be stored in the refrigerator for 2 weeks in a tightly covered container. This is a good recipe to make up ahead of time and have on hand for unexpected guests.

YEAST BREADS

MY FAVORITE ROLL DOUGH

Soften yeast in water—add a pinch of sugar. Melt margarine and add milk, to cool the margarine a little. Beat 2 eggs, and the sugar, milk, and margarine. Add the yeast and the flour, and beat with a wooden spoon until smooth. Let rise until doubled in bulk.

Grease your hands. Turn out onto a floured paper towel. Take ½ of the dough and roll into a circle, using enough flour to keep the dough from sticking to the paper towel and to the rolling pin. You can use a little flour to make the dough a bit stiffer, but you want this dough to be quite soft.

Using a pizza cutter or knife, cut the dough into pie-shaped quarters, then each quarter into thirds. Roll up the dough beginning with the wide part and place on a well-greased cookie sheet. Let rise for about 45 minutes and bake in a 350° oven for 15 minutes or just until light brown.

Repeat the process with the other half of the dough, or roll out this half and spread with about 2 tablespoons butter, some sugar (about ¼ cup), and a generous sprinkling of cinnamon. Add chopped nuts, raisins, or other fruit if you like. Then roll up jelly-roll fashion and with a knife, slice into ½ inch rolls and place on a well-greased cookie sheet and let rise as above. Bake at 350° for 20 minutes. Frost if you like with a powdered sugar icing. I sometimes use a little orange juice as the liquid for the icing.

WHOLE WHEAT BREAD

Combine water and yeast and let set 5 minutes. Add the oil or butter. Then add the whole wheat flour, mixing after each addition. Use dough hooks in your mixer if you have them. Add the molasses and brown sugar and continue beating until mixture is smooth and elastic. Let rise for an hour or until it is almost doubled in bulk. Then add 2 or 3 cups white flour, kneading and working in by hand until the dough is very stiff. Be sure to grease your hands. Let rise one more time and divide into 3 portions; place in well-greased bread pans and let rise for about an hour. Bake in pre-heated oven at 350° for about 45 minutes or until nicely browned and has a hollow sound when you tap with your fingernail.

3 cups warm water
3 packages yeast
¼ cup oil or butter
4 cups whole wheat
  flour
½ cup molasses
¼ cup brown sugar
  (add more to taste)
2 or 3 cups white flour

JIFFY HAMBURGER BUNS

Stir together 2 cups of flour and the yeast. Heat milk, water, oil, sugar, and salt to warm (120° to 130°). Add liquid at once to flour and yeast mixture. Beat until smooth, about 3 minutes on medium speed, or 300 strokes by hand.

Add enough flour to make a soft dough. Mix well. Let mixture rest for 10 minutes. Roll out on floured surface to ½-inch thickness. Cut with 3-inch round cutter or 1-pound coffee can. Place rounds on greased baking sheet. Let rise until the dough doubles in size. Bake for 12 to 15 minutes at 400° to 425°.

4½ to 5 cups flour
2 packages dry yeast
1 cup milk
¾ cup water
½ cup oil
¼ cup sugar
1 tablespoon salt

NEVER FAIL CINNAMON ROLLS

Dissolve yeast in lukewarm water. Add sugar, eggs, and 3 cups of the flour. Beat well. Let rise in warm place for 1 hour.

Add shortening, salt, and remaining flour. Roll out to ¼-inch thickness. Spread with melted butter, sprinkle well with brown sugar, sprinkle with cinnamon. Roll into a long roll and slice 1 inch to 1½ inches thick. Place in greased pan and let rise for ½ hour. Bake 15-20 minutes at 350°. Spread with powdered sugar, milk, and butter icing.

2 packages yeast
¼ cup warm water
½ cup sugar
2 eggs, beaten
6 cups flour
4 tablespoons
  shortening
1 teaspoon salt
1¾ cups scalded milk—
  cooled to lukewarm

PHYL'S PIZZA DOUGH

Place Crisco and salt in a bowl and pour boiling water over them. Stir and allow to cool. In another bowl, crumble yeast into warm water and stir till dissolved. Add to the Crisco mixture. Now add flour and mix well. Knead 10 minutes.

Add more flour if necessary. Allow to rise for 30 minutes. Refrigerate overnight or until well-chilled, or freeze half and refrigerate half.

Grease pizza pans and sprinkle lightly with corn meal. With

2 tablespoons Crisco
⅛ teaspoon salt
1 cup boiling water
1 yeast cake (or 1
  package dry yeast)
¼ cup warm water
3 cups flour
Corn meal

greased hands spread dough to fit pans. Fill with your favorite pizza ingredients and sauce. Bake at 425° to 450° for 15 minutes or until brown and bubbly. Makes 2 large crusts or 4 small.

Cakes, Frostings, Cookies, and Desserts

CAKES

SHORTCAKE

Mix dry ingredients thoroughly; cut in shortening. Make small well in center of flour and pour in egg and milk. Mix with fork until blended. Drop by heaping tablespoons onto greased cookie sheet. Bake in hot oven (450°) 12-15 minutes. While hot, remove tops carefully with fork, butter generously and return tops immediately. When all are buttered, put strawberries on bottom half; replace top, add more berries and whipped cream. Serves 6 to 8.

2 cups flour
1 tablespoon baking powder
3 tablespoons sugar
¾ teaspoon salt
½ cup shortening
1 slightly beaten egg
½ cup milk

LEMON CAKE SUPREME

Mix together, beat well. Bake 40 minutes in 350° oven. While cake is baking, mix powdered sugar and lemonade. Remove cake from oven when done and make tiny holes in top of cake with a fork. Pour icing over cake, smooth evenly and let set. This is a lovely moist cake that will remain fresh for several days.

1 lemon cake mix
1 3-ounce package lemon Jell-O
¾ cup salad oil
¾ cup water
4 eggs
Icing:
2 cups powdered sugar
½ cup frozen lemonade

PINEAPPLE UPSIDE-DOWN CAKE

Cream butter and sugar; add eggs and flavoring and beat well. Sift dry ingredients together and add alternately with milk. Beat until smooth.

Put ¼ cup butter and 1 cup brown sugar in well-greased 9" x 9" cake pan. Cover with sliced drained pineapple with maraschino cherry in center of each, for color. Cover with batter and bake 45 minutes in 350° oven. When cake springs lightly when touched with finger, remove from oven and place upside-down on foil sheet. (A small white or yellow cake mix may be used for the batter.) Serve with whipped cream. Serves 9.

¼ cup butter
¾ cup sugar
1 egg
1 teaspoon vanilla
¼ teaspoon salt
1½ cups flour
2 teaspoons baking powder
½ cup milk

APPLE CAKE

1 cup white sugar
1 cup brown sugar
½ cup shortening
2 eggs
1 cup milk
2½ cups flour
1 teaspoon salt
1 teaspoon baking
 powder
1 teaspoon baking soda
2 cups diced apples

Cream together sugars, shortening, eggs, and milk. Sift dry ingredients and add to creamed mixture. Fold in apples. Pour into greased 9″ x 13″ pan or two 8″ x 8″ pans.

Sprinkle ½ cup white sugar and ½ cup nuts over top.

Bake 40 minutes at 375°. Serve with whipped cream or ice cream, or plain, as a coffee cake.

BETTY'S BANANA CAKE

½ cup shortening
1½ cups sugar
2 large eggs
2 cups flour
¼ teaspoon baking
 powder
¾ teaspoon baking soda
1 teaspoon salt
¼ cup buttermilk (or
 add 1 teaspoon
 vinegar to ¼ cup milk
 if you don't have
 buttermilk)
1 cup mashed bananas
½ cup chopped nuts

Cream together shortening, sugar, and eggs. Add sifted dry ingredients. Stir in buttermilk, bananas, and nuts. Bake in greased and floured 9″ x 13″ pan at 350° 25 to 30 minutes. Frost with burned butter frosting.

MAYONNAISE CAKE

1 cup mayonnaise
1 cup sugar
¼ cup cocoa
1 cup warm water
1 teaspoon vanilla
2 cups flour
2 teaspoons baking soda

Mix together mayonnaise, sugar, and cocoa. Add the water, vanilla, flour, and baking soda. Mix thoroughly and bake in 9″ x 13″ pan at 350° 30 to 40 minutes.

ROBERTA'S SOUR CREAM CAKE

3 eggs
½ cup cocoa
½ cup boiling water
1 teaspoon baking soda
1¾ cups sugar
1⅞ cups flour
1 cup sour cream
1 teaspoon vanilla

Beat eggs and a pinch of salt until light and fluffy. Add cocoa, water, and baking soda. Mix well. Then add sugar, flour, sour cream, and vanilla. Turn into greased and floured 9″ x 13″ or two 8″ x 8″ pans and bake at 350° 30 minutes.

JO'S PINEAPPLE-FILLED ANGEL FOOD CAKE

Bake one angel food cake according to the directions on the package. Cool, remove from pan, slice horizontally into 3 thick slices. Top each with filling and put cake back together. Refrigerate. This is a dessert that can be refrigerated and served a day or two later. It keeps well.

Pineapple Filling

Beat together 2 eggs and 1 cup of sugar. Add 2 tablespoons flour and 1 small can crushed pineapple with juice. Cook, stirring constantly until thickened. Cool completely. Fold in 1 cup whipped cream.

FRESH APPLE CAKE

Pour sugar over apples; mix and let stand while preparing rest of ingredients. Add oil, eggs, vanilla, and nuts to apples. Sift together dry ingredients and add to apple mixture. Stir together and pour into greased and floured 9" x 13" pan. Bake 45 minutes at 350°. Cool and serve with whipped cream or vanilla ice cream. This may be made a day before as it is moist and keeps well. Serves 12 to 15.

4 cups diced fresh apples (peeled)
2 cups white sugar
½ cup cooking oil
2 well-beaten eggs
2 teaspoons vanilla
1 cup nuts
2 cups flour
2 teaspoons baking soda
2 teaspoons cinnamon
1 teaspoon salt

PEACH UPSIDE-DOWN CAKE

Melt butter; add brown sugar and stir until blended. Pour into 8" x 8" pan and set aside.

Sift together dry ingredients. In separate bowl, cream shortening and sugar. Stir in beaten egg and vanilla. Add dry ingredients alternately with milk to shortening mixture.

Layer peaches over brown sugar in the pan; top with batter. Bake at 350° for 40 minutes. Serve with whipped cream or ice cream.

Note: Substitute two 12-ounce packages of defrosted, drained peaches if fresh ones aren't available.

¼ cup butter
½ cup brown sugar
1¼ teaspoons baking powder
¼ teaspoon salt
1 cup plus 2 teaspoons flour
¼ cup shortening
¾ cup sugar
1 egg, beaten
1 teaspoon vanilla
½ cup milk
2 cups ripe peaches, sliced

RUTH'S CHOCOLATE CUPCAKES

Melt chocolate and margarine; stir in nuts to coat. Combine sugar, flour, eggs and vanilla. Mix until blended, but do not beat. Fold in chocolate-nut mixture. Bake in greased muffin pans at 325° 30 minutes. Cool; remove from pan after 10 minutes to prevent sticking. Do not frost.

4 squares semi-sweet chocolate
2 sticks margarine
¼ teaspoon butter flavoring (optional)
1 cup chopped pecans
1¾ cups sugar
1 cup flour
4 eggs
1 teaspoon vanilla

DATE CHOCOLATE CHIP CAKE

Combine dates, water, and baking soda. Set aside.

In separate bowl, cream together shortening, sugar, and eggs. Stir in date mixture. Sift together dry ingredients and add to the batter. Turn into 9" x 13" pan or two 8" x 8" pans. Mix together the sugar, chocolate chips, and nuts. Spread over cake batter. Bake for 30 minutes at 350°.

1 cup chopped dates
1½ cups boiling water
1 teaspoon baking soda
½ cup shortening
1 cup sugar
2 eggs, well beaten
1¼ cups plus 3 tablespoons flour
¾ teaspoon baking soda
½ cup sugar
1 cup chocolate chips
½ cup chopped nuts

CARROT CAKE

3 cups flour
2 teaspoons baking soda
2 teaspoons cinnamon
2 teaspoons baking powder
1½ cups oil
4 eggs
2 cups grated carrots
1 cup nuts

Combine all the ingredients and bake in a well-greased and floured pan at 350° for 65 to 70 minutes. Remove from pan. Frost with Cream Cheese Frosting (recipe follows).

TEXAS SHEET CAKE by Jan

2 sticks (1 cup) margarine
¼ cup cocoa
1 cup water
2 cups flour
2 cups sugar
½ cup buttermilk (or ½ cup milk + 2 teasp. vinegar)
1 teaspoon baking soda
1 teaspoon cinnamon
1 teaspoon vanilla

Melt margarine, add cocoa and water and bring to a boil. Add flour, sugar, buttermilk, soda, cinnamon, and vanilla. Mix well and pour into 9″ x 13″ pan. Bake 20 minutes at 400°.

Topping

½ cup margarine
¼ cup cocoa
6 tablespoons milk
1 lb. powdered sugar
1 teaspoon vanilla
½ cup walnuts

While sheet cake is baking, mix ingredients for topping. Bring to a boil and remove from heat. Pour over top of cake as soon as you remove it from the oven.

CAKE FROSTINGS

CREAM CHEESE FROSTING

Whip 1 package softened Philadelphia cream cheese and 1 tablespoon milk or cream. Add powdered sugar until of spreading consistency.

BURNED BUTTER FROSTING

Brown slightly in small saucepan 2 tablespoons margarine or butter; add 2 tablespoons milk and 1 teaspoon vanilla. Add enough powdered sugar to thicken to spreading consistency.

CHOCOLATE FROSTING

2 tablespoons butter or margarine, melted
2 tablespoons cocoa
2 tablespoons milk

Combine butter, cocoa, and milk. Add enough powdered sugar to thicken to spreading consistency.

BUTTER FROSTING

⅓ cup (⅔ stick) margarine
3 to 4 tablespoons milk or cream
1 pound package powdered sugar
1 teaspoon vanilla

Soften margarine by placing it in bowl in warm water. Add 2 tablespoons milk alternately with the powdered sugar, stirring until smooth. Add vanilla and as much more milk as needed to bring frosting to desired smoothness for spreading. Add 2 rounded tablespoons cocoa, or more if desired, to make chocolate icing.

COOKIES

RICE KRISPIES SQUARES

Melt butter and marshmallows in pan over low heat, stirring constantly. Bring to rolling boil and boil 1 minute. Remove from heat. Put Rice Krispies in large, greased pan. Pour on hot marshmallow mixture; stir until well coated. Pour into well-buttered 9" x 13" pan and pat down well with buttered spoon. Cool in refrigerator. Cut into squares and serve.

¼ pound (1 stick) butter or margarine
30 large marshmallows
5 cups Rice Krispies

WHEAT PUFF CANDY SQUARES

Cook butter, sugar, syrup, and cocoa in pan over medium heat. Bring to rolling boil and boil 1 minute. Remove from heat and add vanilla.

Place Puffed Wheat in large greased pan and pour on hot mixture; stir until cereal is coated. Pour onto buttered cookie sheet and press down with buttered spoon. Cool in refrigerator. Cut into squares.

⅓ cup butter
½ cup light corn syrup
1 cup brown sugar
2 tablespoons cocoa
1 teaspoon vanilla
8 cups Puffed Wheat

THUMBPRINT COOKIES

Combine ingredients and roll between palms of hands into balls the size of a walnut. Dip in beaten whites of 2 eggs, then in chopped nuts. Press down slightly on cookie sheet. Bake in 350° oven 5 minutes. Remove from oven and immediately make small, thumbprint-like impression on top of each cookie. Bake 8 minutes more. Cool and fill depression with colored powdered sugar icing.

1 cup butter
½ cup brown sugar
2 egg yolks
1 teaspoon vanilla
¼ teaspoon salt
2 cups flour

ROLLED SOUR CREAM COOKIES

Cream shortening and sugar; add egg and beat well. Add dry ingredients, sour cream, and vanilla. Stir well. Turn onto floured surface and roll ½-inch thick. Cut in various shapes and bake until just done (about 10-12 minutes) in 375° oven. Do not brown. Sprinkle sugar lightly on top just before baking, if desired.

½ cup shortening
1 cup sugar
1 egg
½ teaspoon salt
1½ teaspoons baking powder
¼ teaspoon baking soda
1 teaspoon vanilla
2¾ cups flour
½ cup sour cream

ORANGE NUT CRISPS

Cream sugar and margarine; add egg yolk, flour, orange and lemon rinds. Use hands to work in thoroughly. Roll into walnut-sized balls. Dip in slightly-beaten egg white, then in chopped nuts. Place on greased cookie sheet and flatten slightly with fork. Bake at 350° 15 minutes.

½ cup sugar
⅓ cup margarine
1 cup flour
Grated rind of 1 orange
Grated rind of 1 lemon
1 egg
¾ cup finely chopped nuts

CHOCOLATE CHIP OATMEAL CRISPS

1 cup margarine
1 cup white sugar
2 eggs
1 teaspoon baking soda
½ teaspoon salt
1½ cups flour
2 cups quick oatmeal
½ cup chocolate chips
½ cup nuts
1 teaspoon cinnamon

Cream margarine and sugar; beat in eggs. Add soda, salt, and flour and mix thoroughly. Add oatmeal, chips, nuts, and cinnamon. Stir well. Drop by teaspoons on ungreased cookie sheet. Bake until golden brown in 350° oven 10 to 15 minutes.

BROWNIES

½ cup margarine
1 cup sugar
2 eggs
¼ cup cocoa
1 cup flour
¼ cup milk
Dash salt
1 teaspoon vanilla
½ cup chopped nuts

Cream margarine and sugar, add eggs; combine cocoa with enough hot water to make a paste and add to above ingredients. Beat in flour and milk alternately. Add salt, vanilla, and nuts; mix well. Spread in shallow, greased 9" x 13" pan and bake 20 minutes at 375°. Frost while warm with chocolate powdered sugar frosting. Cut into squares when cool.

SNICKERDOODLES

1 cup margarine
1½ cups sugar
2 eggs
½ teaspoon salt
1 teaspoon baking soda
2 teaspoons cream of
  tartar
2¾ cups flour

Cream margarine and sugar; add eggs and mix well. Add dry ingredients. Chill dough and roll into walnut-sized balls. Roll in a mixture of 2 tablespoons sugar and 2 teaspoons cinnamon. Place on cookie sheet; bake in 400° oven 10 minutes, or until golden brown.

EVELYN'S BONBON COOKIES

1 8-ounce package
  cream cheese
1 cup soft butter or
  margarine
2 cups flour
Walnut halves or dates

Mix cheese and butter with fork. Work in flour with hands. Chill mixture in refrigerator. Roll dough ⅛-inch thick on surface sprinkled heavily with powdered sugar. Cut dough in strips 1" x 3". Put walnut half (or date) on each and roll up. Place folded side down on cookie sheet; bake 10-15 minutes in 350° oven. Sprinkle warm cookies with powdered sugar.

AUNT JO'S SUGAR COOKIES

½ cup butter
½ cup shortening
½ cup white sugar
½ cup brown sugar
1 egg
1 teaspoon vanilla
2¼ cups flour
½ teaspoon salt
2 teaspoons cream of tartar
1 teaspoon baking soda

Cream butter, shortening, and sugar; add remaining ingredients in order given. Roll into balls and flatten. Bake at 350° until just done, not brown. Roll in powdered sugar or frost. Add nuts to batter if desired.

CHOCOLATE KRISPIES COOKIES

Cook sugar and syrup in saucepan over medium heat, stirring constantly until it reaches the boiling point. Remove from heat and stir in peanut butter; mix well. Add cereal and press into buttered 9" x 13" pan. Top with melted chocolate chips spread evenly. Cool until firm and cut into bars.

1 cup sugar
1 cup light corn syrup
1 cup peanut butter
6 cups Rice Krispies
1 cup chocolate chips

DESSERTS

RASPBERRY FLUFF

Put gelatin into blender; add boiling water, cover, and blend 2 minutes to dissolve. Slowly add ice while blending one minute, or until blender feels cool. Pour into *chilled* sherbet glasses. Serve in five minutes. Trim with fresh berries or whipped cream if desired.

1 3-ounce package raspberry gelatin
½ cup boiling water
1 cup drained, crushed ice

LOIS'S BLUEBERRY DESSERT

Crush crackers fine, add melted butter and ½ cup sugar. Blend and press into 11" x 15" pan. Beat eggs, cream cheese, 1 cup sugar, and vanilla until smooth. Spread over cracker layer and bake 25 minutes at 325°. When cooled, spread with blueberry filling. Chill and serve with whipped cream. This is a large recipe which keeps well.

28 square graham crackers
½ cup melted butter
½ cup sugar
4 eggs
2 8-ounce packages cream cheese
1 cup sugar
1½ teaspoons vanilla
2 cans blueberry pie filling

FRUIT NUT DESSERT

In saucepan over low heat, stir marshmallows and margarine until nearly melted; cool until partially thickened.

Combine eggs, sugar, lemon juice, and salt in top of double boiler and cook over boiling water, stirring constantly until thick. Remove from heat and add marshmallow mixture. Fold in the pineapple, cherries, pecans, and whipped cream.

Pour into 8" x 8" pan and chill until firm. Serves 8 to 10.

¼ cup margarine
2 cups miniature marshmallows
2 beaten eggs
2 tablespoons sugar
⅓ cup lemon juice
Pinch of salt
1 small can drained pineapple chunks
1 medium-sized can pitted bing cherries, drained
1 cup chopped pecans
1 cup cream, whipped

MARSHMALLOW PARFAIT

Melt marshmallows in milk in top of double boiler, or on top of stove at very low heat, stirring constantly. Cool and add fruit. Fold in whipped cream and put in parfait glasses. Freeze 2 hours. Serves 6 to 8.

2 cups miniature marshmallows
3 tablespoons milk
1 cup fresh strawberries or raspberries, crushed
1 cup cream, whipped

ANGEL FOOD DESSERT

3 cups milk, scalded
Pinch of salt
4 eggs, separated
1 cup sugar
2 envelopes unflavored
  gelatin
2 cups cream, whipped
1 angel food loaf cake
1 small can crushed
  pineapple
½ cup maraschino
  cherries
½ cup nuts, chopped

Beat egg yolks and sugar together; add salt and milk. Bring to boil over medium heat; remove from stove. Dissolve gelatin in 3 tablespoons cold water; add to above ingredients. Cool and fold in stiffly beaten egg whites. Let stand until set. Fold in whipped cream.

Break cake into 1-inch pieces. Using a 9″ x 13″ pan, put in a layer of cake crumbs, a layer of the custard mixture, a layer of drained pineapple, cherries, and nuts. Repeat, ending with fruit and nuts. Note: This is a large dessert and could be halved successfully although it keeps well. Serve plain or with whipped cream. Delicious!

PINEAPPLE DELIGHT

1 pound marshmallows
¾ cup milk
1 small can crushed
  pineapple
1 pint cream, whipped
24 square graham
  crackers

Melt marshmallows in milk over low heat, stirring constantly. Cool. Add pineapple with juice. Fold in whipped cream. Crush graham crackers with rolling pin. Line 9″ x 13″ pan with cracker crumbs, saving ½ cup for topping. Pour filling in slowly, sprinkle crumbs on top, and refrigerate 3 to 4 hours. Serves 12.

SURPRISE PEACH PUDDING

½ cup sugar
1 cup flour
2 teaspoons baking powder
½ cup milk
2 cups diced peaches
½ cup brown sugar
½ cup white sugar
2 cups water
1 tablespoon butter or
  margarine

Combine sugar, flour, and baking powder in mixing bowl; add milk and peaches. Stir lightly, then spread in well-greased 8″ x 8″ square pan.

Combine sugars, water, and butter in saucepan. Heat to boiling point, stirring to dissolve sugar. Pour over batter in pan. Bake in 400° oven 45 minutes. Serve warm or chilled, with whipped cream. There will be a delicious sauce on the bottom and a crusty topping.

MY FAVORITE APPLE CRISP

½ cup white sugar
½ cup brown sugar
¾ cup flour
¼ cup butter or
  margarine
4 cups apples, sliced
  thick
¼ cup water
1 teaspoon cinnamon

Work sugars, flour, and butter together with fingers until crumbly. Pare apples and slice into greased, shallow pan. Pour water over apples and generously sprinkle with cinnamon. Spread crumb mixture over apples and bake uncovered 50 minutes at 350°. Serve warm with whipped cream, a wedge of cheese, or with ice cream.

EVELYN'S PUMPKIN PARFAIT DESSERT

1½ cups graham
  crackers, rolled fine
¼ cup sugar
1 cup canned pumpkin
¼ cup brown sugar
½ teaspoon salt
½ teaspoon cinnamon
½ teaspoon ginger
¼ teaspoon nutmeg
1 quart vanilla ice cream

Combine cracker crumbs and white sugar and spread a thin layer in an 8″ x 8″ pan. Mix pumpkin, brown sugar, salt, and spices. Fold in ice cream. Alternate layers of pumpkin mixture and crackers. Freeze. This keeps well.

SIMPLE FRUIT PARFAITS

Peel and slice fresh fruit as needed. Spoon into parfait glasses alternately with ice cream, allowing ¼ cup fruit per glass. Prepare parfaits and place in freezer 30 minutes before using. Raspberries, strawberries, blueberries, sweet cherries, peaches, or cantaloupe balls may be used. If fruit is tart, marshmallow creme topping may be alternated with ice cream to add sweetness.

When repairing broken china, tape one side to hold until the glue dries completely.

MOTHER'S BREAD PUDDING

Mix together all ingredients and place in baking dish. Dot with butter and bake 40 to 50 minutes at 350°.

2 cups milk
4 cups bread crumbs
¼ cup melted margarine
2 beaten eggs
½ cup sugar
½ teaspoon salt
1 teaspoon cinnamon
½ cup raisins

CHOCOLATE CREAM PIE

Put in saucepan: 1 package chocolate pudding mix, 2 lightly beaten egg yolks, ¾ cup evaporated milk, and ¾ cup water. Bring to boil over low heat, stirring constantly. Let boil slowly ½ minute, remove from stove, cover, and cool thoroughly. Pour into 9″ baked pie shell. Beat whites of 2 eggs until stiff while slowly adding ½ cup sugar. Spread meringue over filling to edge of crust. Brown in moderate (325°) oven 15 minutes.

PECAN PIE

Prepare pastry for a single-crust pie; do not prick or bake.

Cream butter, vanilla, sugar, and eggs; beat well. Add chopped pecans. Pour into unbaked pastry shell and bake 10 minutes in 450° oven. Reduce heat to 350° and sprinkle remaining pecan halves on top. Bake 30 to 35 minutes longer. Cool and serve plain or with whipped cream.

3 tablespoons butter
1 teaspoon vanilla
¾ cup sugar
3 eggs
1 cup dark corn syrup
⅛ teaspoon salt
⅔ cup chopped pecans
⅓ cup whole pecan halves

COCONUT PECAN PIE

Beat egg whites and vinegar until stiff. Add sugar and vanilla and beat well. Add nuts, coconut, crackers, and baking powder. Pour batter into 8″ greased pie pan. Bake 30 minutes in 350° oven. Top with whipped cream.

4 egg whites
1 teaspoon vinegar
1 cup sugar
1 teaspoon vanilla
½ cup pecans, chopped
¼ cup shredded coconut
10 graham crackers, rolled fine
1 teaspoon baking powder

Don't . . . don't . . . don't prick unbaked pie shell if it is to be filled before baking. Only prick a shell if it is to be baked first and a cream filling added later.

APPLE PIE

Prepare pastry for double-crust pie and roll out. Combine 2 tablespoons flour with 1 cup sugar; sprinkle ¼ cup into bottom crust. Add enough apples, peeled and sliced, to fill shell; add remaining sugar. Sprinkle generously with cinnamon and dot with butter. Make a few small cuts in top crust (to allow steam to escape), and put over fruit. Seal edges of crust by dipping fingers in water and pinching crust together around edge of pie pan. Cut off excess crust. Bake in 450° oven 15 minutes, then reduce heat to 325° and bake 35 minutes, or until apples are tender.

APPLE-PEAR PIE

¾ cup sugar
2 teaspoons flour
½ teaspoon cinnamon
¼ teaspoon salt
1 teaspoon grated lemon rind
1 tablespoon lemon juice

Peel and halve enough pears to cover bottom of a 9-inch unbaked pie shell. Peel and slice enough apples to fill shell. Mix together sugar, flour, cinnamon, salt, lemon rind, and lemon juice. Sprinkle over fruit in pie shell.

Combine ¼ cup flour, ¼ cup butter, ½ cup brown sugar, ½ teaspoon salt. Cut butter into dry ingredients and mix until crumbly; stir in ½ cup chopped nuts and sprinkle over pie filling. Bake in 400° oven 15 minutes. Cover with foil and bake 25 minutes, or until apples are tender when stuck with a fork. Serve with whipped cream.

PASTRY FOR DOUBLE-CRUST PIE

2 cups flour
⅔ cup plus 1 heaping tablespoon shortening
6 tablespoons cold water
1 teaspoon salt

Measure flour and salt into bowl; add shortening; blend with fingers until mixture resembles coarse meal. Add water and mix gently with spoon or fork. Roll half the dough on floured surface until a little larger than pie pan. Place crust in pan, but do not trim. Fill as directed in recipe. Roll out remainder of dough, pierce with knife several places, and place over filling. (Moistening the rim of the bottom crust with your fingers will help to seal edges.) Trim excess dough and pinch to seal. Bake pie in hot oven (450°) to prevent soggy crust.

SODA CRACKER CRUST

Brush half-and-half or egg yolk diluted with milk over the top of a two-crust pie. Gives a rich, brown finish.

Beat 3 egg whites until stiff. Add alternately ½ cup sugar mixed with ¼ teaspoon baking powder, 24 soda crackers rolled fine, ½ cup finely chopped nuts, 1 teaspoon vanilla.

Press into buttered pie pan and bake ½ hour at 325°. When ready to serve, fill with drained peaches, pineapple, or fresh, sugared strawberries. Top with whipped cream sweetened with 2 teaspoons powdered sugar.

JAN'S BAVARIAN MINT PIE

Melt butter and pour over crushed wafers. Mix well and press firmly into a 9" pie pan. Chill until set.

Cream butter and sugar until light and fluffy at high speed on mixer. Beat in eggs, one at a time, beating well after each addition. Melt chocolate, add flavoring, and cool. Blend into creamy mixture. Turn into crust. Sprinkle with pecans. Refrigerate until set, about 3 hours.

Crust
1¼ cup vanilla wafers, crushed fine
½ cup butter

Filling
½ cup butter
¾ cup sugar
3 eggs
1 square unsweetened chocolate
1 4-ounce package sweet chocolate bar or chips
¼ teaspoon peppermint flavoring
¼ cup chopped pecans

MYSTERY TORTE

Beat egg whites until stiff. Gradually add sugar as you beat. Add baking powder and vanilla. Fold in crackers and pecans slowly. When mixed, pour into lightly greased 8" pie pan. Bake 30 minutes at 350°. Spread with whipped topping and sprinkle with chocolate curls.

3 egg whites
1 cup sugar
½ teaspoon baking powder
1 teaspoon vanilla
16 Ritz crackers, crushed fine
⅔ cup pecans, chopped

Do you have trouble with a fruit pie boiling over in the oven? Here's one remedy. Tear a strip of clean cloth about 1½ inches wide and long enough to go around the outside rim of the pie plate. Wet the cloth and wrap it around the edge of the pie, lapping it over at the two ends. When the pie is baked, the cloth peels off easily.

Casseroles

TEN

GROUND BEEF BAKE

Brown 1 pound ground beef and ⅓ cup chopped onion. Add ½ teaspoon salt and dash of pepper.

Crush 1 cup potato chips and press onto bottom of 8″ square pan. Cover with several slices American cheese and spoon meat onto cheese. Spread ¼ cup chili sauce over meat. Top with wedges of peeled tomato. Cover tomato with crushed potato chips and bake about 15 minutes at 350°. Serve with scalloped potatoes or baked beans.

MEAL IN ONE

Into casserole slice enough potatoes to serve the number of people. Add a layer of sliced carrots and a layer of chopped cabbage. Place as many hamburger patties as needed on the layer of cabbage and top each with a slice of onion. Dilute 1 can condensed cream of mushroom soup with 1 can milk and pour over all. Cover and bake 1½ to 2 hours in a 300° oven.

MACARONI AND CHEESE

Bring to boil 1 quart of water. Add 1 teaspoon salt. Add 1 package macaroni, stirring slowly. Stir until water comes to boil again; turn down heat. Cook gently until macaroni is tender. Drain macaroni; turn into buttered casserole. Stir in ½ pound of cubed cheese and top with bread crumbs. Cover with milk and bake in pre-heated oven (350°) 25 minutes.

TUNA-EGG CASSEROLE

Simmer celery in water until soft. Add ½ can mushroom soup and blend. Combine tuna, lemon peel, rest of soup, and seasoning. Arrange layers of tuna, chopped eggs, celery, and soup mixture in greased 1 quart casserole. Bake in 450° oven 15 minutes, or until bubbly and brown. Serves 5.

"If you are filled with light within, with no dark corners, then the outside will be radiant too, as though a floodlight is beamed upon you."

LUKE 11:36

Hunger is good—if it makes you work to satisfy it!

PROVERBS 16:26

1 cup chopped celery
½ cup water
1 can mushroom soup
1 can tuna
4 hard-boiled eggs
2 teaspoons grated
    lemon peel
½ teaspoon salt
¼ teaspoon pepper
½ cup grated processed
    cheese

SCALLOPED POTATOES AND SPAM

Slice 4 or 5 medium potatoes into buttered casserole. Top with 1 can Spam, sliced. Add buttered bread crumbs and pour on 2 cups medium white sauce to which 1 tablespoon grated onion has been added. Bake in 350° oven 30 minutes, or until potatoes are tender.

JACK POT CASSEROLE

1 pound hamburger
2 tablespoons
   shortening
¼ cup chopped onion
1 can tomato soup
1½ cups water
½ 8-ounce package
   noodles
Salt and pepper
1 No. 2 can cream style
   corn
1 cup grated processed
   cheese

Melt shortening; add hamburger and onions and brown. Add tomato soup, corn, water, and noodles. Put in greased casserole; top with grated cheese. Bake 45 minutes in 350° oven.

BAKED STEW

1 can tomato soup
1 can mushroom soup
1 pound hamburger
¼ cup diced onions
¼ cup diced celery
Salt and pepper
6 carrots
5 medium potatoes

Mix soups together over low heat. Brown onions, celery, and hamburger in skillet. Pare 6 carrots and 5 medium-sized potatoes; cut into chunks. Alternate layers in baking dish, one layer vegetables, one layer meat mixture, one layer soup mixture. Bake in casserole 1 hour at 350°. Serves 4 to 6.

NOODLES À LA CORNED BEEF

1 8-ounce package
   noodles
1 12-ounce can corned
   beef
¼ pound processed
   cheese, diced
1 12-ounce can chicken
   noodle soup
1 cup milk
¾ cup potato chips or
   bread crumbs
Onions, if desired

Cook noodles, drain. Add corned beef, cheese, soup, milk, and onions; stir gently. Place in greased casserole; top with crumbs and dot with butter. Bake at 350° 45 minutes. Serves 10.

CHICKEN À LA KING

2 cups cold chicken,
   diced
1 cup canned
   mushrooms (drained)
2 slightly-beaten egg
   yolks
2 cups white sauce
2 tablespoons butter

Put cold diced chicken and mushrooms in greased casserole. Add egg yolks to white sauce and stir lightly. Pour white sauce over chicken, stirring gently to penetrate. Top with bread or cracker crumbs, dot with butter. Bake 350° 45 minutes.

Use canned chicken, leftover baked chicken, or chicken you have boiled until the meat is tender and falls from the bone.

SPINACH CASSEROLE

In a 9" x 13" pan, make a layer of the artichoke hearts. You may want to cut them up if the pieces are large. Cook the spinach and drain. Combine with cream cheese and margarine and pour on top of the artichoke hearts. Top with buttered bread crumbs and bake at 350° for 25 minutes.

2 jars marinated artichoke hearts, drained
4 packages frozen, chopped spinach
½ cup margarine
2 8-ounce packages cream cheese
Buttered bread crumbs

BAKED GREEN BEAN CASSEROLE

If you keep one or all of the ingredients in this recipe on hand, you'll always have a nice casserole to serve to guests or to your family. There is some versatility in using ingredients—all of them work out very nicely.

Combine the beans and soup in a 9" x 13" pan and top with onions or almonds. Bake in a 350° oven for about 30 minutes.

3 16-ounce cans green beans (I prefer the French cut)
1 can cheddar cheese soup, cream of mushroom soup, or cream of celery soup
1 can onion rings or ½ cup sliced toasted almonds

CABBAGE CASSEROLE

Chop cabbage, cook until tender, and drain. Brown ground beef and onion. Drain beef and combine with cabbage. Add salt and pepper to taste. Put in a 2½-quart casserole and top with cheese and cracker crumbs. Bake at 350° for 30 minutes.

1 head cabbage
1 pound ground beef
1 small onion, chopped
¾ cup sharp cheese, grated
½ cup cracker crumbs
Salt and pepper to taste

GOULASH

Brown these ingredients in an electric skillet at 350°. Add 3½ cups noodles, uncooked. Mix together 2½ cups tomato juice, 2 teaspoons Worcestershire sauce, 1 teaspoon celery salt, 1 can condensed beef broth, ½ cup water.

Pour over noodles. Cover and cook 12 to 15 minutes or until noodles are tender, stirring occasionally. Stir in ⅔ cup drained, broiled mushrooms (optional) and 1 cup sour cream. Heat. Serves 4.

1 pound ground beef
1 cup chopped onion
1 clove garlic, minced
1 teaspoon salt

SKILLET DINNER

Line a skillet with two slices of bacon cut in one-inch pieces. Add four or more hamburger patties, depending on the number of people to serve. Top with three or four sliced potatoes and three or four sliced carrots. If you like onion, put a slice on each hamburger patty. Cover skillet and put on high heat until the bacon sizzles (about one minute). Add ¼ cup water and lower the heat. Cook about 30 minutes or until tender.

If you want to lift someone who is down, you have to get on your knees.

Eggs

ELEVEN

BOILED

Set eggs out of refrigerator several hours or overnight. Cover with warm water and bring to a boil. Boil 3 minutes for soft and 7 minutes for hard-cooked egg. If you must use eggs directly from the refrigerator, place them in a pan of lukewarm water for 5 to 10 minutes before boiling to prevent cracking.

FRIED

Fry bacon to crisp in a moderately hot skillet, spoon out all but 2 or 3 tablespoons fat. Break eggs one at a time into a saucer, then pour each egg carefully into the skillet; add salt and pepper. Place a tight lid on the pan for 3 or 4 minutes for a medium well-done egg, or spoon bacon fat over the egg until the white is cooked. For a hard-fried egg, turn carefully with a pancake turner after the white is well cooked and leave until the yolk is hard. Two tablespoons butter or margarine may be used for fat, but fry more slowly as these fats burn quickly. Serve hot.

STEAMED

Prepare pan as above but leave only enough fat to coat the skillet. Add 1 teaspoon water for each egg; cover immediately. Cook to desired firmness. Serve hot.

POACHED

Using an egg poacher with cups, place 1 cup hot water in lower pan and bring to boil; reduce heat. Place rack and buttered cups into pan. Break 1 egg into each cup; add salt and pepper, cover tightly. Cook 3 to 6 minutes. Test with fork occasionally for desired hardness.

SCRAMBLED

Break one or two eggs for each serving, first into cup, and then into mixing bowl. Add salt and pepper and 1½ tablespoons milk for each egg. Beat slightly with fork. Put 2 tablespoons bacon fat or shortening into skillet on medium high heat. Pour eggs into skillet. When

Improvise a stove mat by covering an old magazine with foil. You will be able to lay knives and spoons on this while cooking. It wipes clean in a jiffy.

they begin to turn white on the bottom, turn lightly with a spatula until all the egg is cooked, 4 to 7 minutes. Do not allow the eggs to cook too long as this makes them dry and hard.

Add small pieces of dried beef or crisp bacon to scrambled eggs to make the basis of a tasty quick lunch.

BACON AND EGG CUPS
Grease muffin tins; line the cup with one strip of bacon, standing it up and overlapping if too long. Break an egg into each. Dot with butter, salt and pepper. Add 1 teaspoon milk or cream to each if desired. Bake in 350° oven 15 to 18 minutes.

CREAMED EGGS
Prepare hard-cooked eggs. Peel and dice. Add to white sauce and serve over hot buttered toast or on fluffy cooked rice.

WHITE SAUCE
Melt 1 tablespoon butter in pan and add 1 tablespoon flour, ¼ teaspoon salt, dash of pepper. Stir together; add 1 cup milk slowly and bring to boil 1 minute stirring constantly. Remove from stove and stir in diced eggs gently; serve hot.

EGG BREAKFAST CASSEROLE

12 slices bread, cubed
1 pound cheese, diced
2 cups ham, diced
½ cup margarine, melted
6-7 eggs
1 quart milk
½ teaspoon salt
Pinch of pepper
1 teaspoon dry mustard

Place bread cubes in greased pan. Add a layer of cheese and a layer of ham. Pour melted margarine over all. Blend eggs, milk, salt, pepper, and mustard and pour over all. Refrigerate overnight. In morning bake 1 hour at 350°.

IMPOSSIBLE QUICHE

3 eggs
½ cup Bisquick
⅓ cup melted margarine
1½ cups milk
⅛ teaspoon each of pepper and salt
1¼ cups shredded swiss cheese
⅓ cup ham, bacon, shrimp, or crab meat

Put all ingredients together in a bowl. Mix on high speed for one minute. Pour into a well-greased 9″ pie tin. Bake at 350° for 45 minutes. Let set 5 minutes and serve hot.

When your brow gets wrinkled from worry and care, you need a "faith" lift.

International Dishes

TWELVE

PAULA'S MANICOTTI

Combine first 10 ingredients to make sauce. Simmer for one hour.

Mix cheeses with egg and seasonings. Cook manicotti as directed on package. The pasta should be tender, but not too soft to work with. Cool in cool water, drain, and stuff with cheese mixture. Pour about half of the sauce over all and bake in a large pan or roaster at 350° for ½ hour. Serve with remaining sauce.

This is very tasty with or without the meat.

2 1-pound cans chopped tomatoes
1 6-ounce can tomato sauce
1 6-ounce can tomato paste
1 tablespoon oregano
1 teaspoon rosemary
1 teaspoon thyme
1 tablespoon parsley
1½ cups chopped onion
1 clove garlic, chopped
1 pound ground beef, browned (optional)
1 pound ricotta cheese
8 ounces mozzarella cheese
2 eggs
½ cup parmesan cheese
Salt, pepper, and parsley to taste
1 package manicotti

ITALIAN SPAGHETTI

Lightly brown onion and garlic in fat; add hamburger and tomato paste. Cook slowly until meat is done, 25 to 30 minutes. Put into saucepan and add tomatoes, tomato soup, chili powder, and cinnamon. Cover and simmer 1½ hours. 20 minutes before serving time, cook two 7-ounce packages of spaghetti in boiling water; drain. Place spaghetti on platter, making space in center for sauce. Sprinkle sauce with ½ cup chopped olives and/or Parmesan cheese. Serve with a green salad and you have your meal! Serves 4 to 6.

2 tablespoons salad oil
½ tablespoon minced garlic
1 cup chopped onion
1 small can tomato paste
1 pound hamburger
1 can tomato soup
½ teaspoon cinnamon
2 tablespoons chili powder
1 No. 2 can tomatoes

JAPANESE EGGPLANT

Wash eggplant, slice very thin but do not peel. Flour both sides of each slice. Mix together the hamburger, egg, bread crumbs, garlic, and milk. Mix ingredients well. Make a sandwich of two slices of eggplant and the meat mixture. Flour the meat-filled sandwich again, dip in beaten egg, then in fine dry bread crumbs. Fry in deep fat until evenly browned on both sides. Serve with a sauce made of ½ cup catsup, 1 teaspoon soy sauce, 1 teaspoon sugar, and salt and pepper.

1 pound hamburger
1 egg
½ cup soft bread crumbs
Garlic to taste
½ cup milk (or more if needed to mix easily)

NORIMICHI'S SUKIYAKI

3 bunches green onions, sliced in 2-inch long pieces
3 medium-sized dry onions, quartered
3 carrots, sliced thin, then parboiled 10 minutes
2 pounds beef, sliced in thin pieces (by butcher)
1 small can mushrooms with juice
1 medium-sized can bean sprouts
1 package spinach, thawed
Cooked rice to serve 4

Place 2 tablespoons cooking oil and ¾ cup water in skillet. Add meat one piece at a time. Place onions in one corner of pan, dividing the green and the dry. Add bean sprouts, carrots, and spinach, keeping each separated. Add 1 or 2 tablespoons soy sauce to taste. Cook on medium heat 5 to 10 minutes, being careful not to overcook vegetables. Serve over rice.

VERNA'S CHOW MEIN

2 pounds stew meat, cubed (use part beef, part pork)
2 tablespoons fat
1 large onion, diced
1 cup celery, diced
1 cup water
3 tablespoons sugar
¼ cup soy sauce
1 can chow mein vegetables
1 can bean sprouts
2 tablespoons flour
Salt

Brown meat in fat with onions and celery; add water and simmer 15 minutes. Add sugar, soy sauce, drained vegetables, and drained bean sprouts. Simmer 1 hour or longer, adding more water if necessary. Thicken with flour, and salt to taste. Serve with Chinese noodles.

To remove burned food from aluminum pans, fill pan with cold water, add ¼ cup vinegar and bring to a slow boil. Simmer 10-15 minutes.

Fruits and Vegetables

THIRTEEN

FRUITS

RAW FRUIT

The fruit should be fully ripe and at the peak of beauty. Most berries have their finest flavor when they have been taken from the refrigerator just long enough to be cool, but not cold, and sprinkled with sugar a few minutes before serving. This draws out enough juice to make the fruit most palatable. Cantaloupe and muskmelon are most flavorful when they are at room temperature when served. Watermelon is usually preferred chilled.

Peaches, bananas, and pears are best when peeled and sliced directly into the serving dish and served with a sprinkling of sugar and some cream. Peaches are delicious sugared and chilled so that the sugar may penetrate the fruit. Bananas are best served at room temperature; pears may be served either way.

Fresh pineapple requires special attention. A small amount of sugar makes the fruit juicier and more enjoyable.

Apples, pears, peach halves, and grapes may be eaten with the fingers or attractively arranged and served from a fruit bowl. When served with a variety of cheese and several kinds of crackers, a fruit plate or bowl is a simple but satisfying dessert.

STEWED PRUNES

Wash dried prunes in cold water. Place in saucepan and barely cover with lukewarm water. Allow to soak 1 to 2 hours, then cook slowly in the same water over low heat until the fruit is tender. Sugar need not be added, though a small amount gives a thicker and more attractive syrup. Chill before serving.

BROILED GRAPEFRUIT

Cut grapefruit in half across the middle. Remove the seeds and cut around the outer edge of the fruit and along the sections with a sharp knife. Sprinkle each half with 1 tablespoon brown sugar. Place under broiler until sugar is melted and the edges of the grapefruit are a light brown. Remove from oven and serve at once.

"Yes, the way to identify a tree or a person is by the kind of fruit produced."
MATTHEW 7:20

GRAPEFRUIT ICE

Combine 2 cups sugar with 4 cups water. Bring to boil and boil 10 minutes; cool. Add 2 cups canned bite-sized grapefruit sections and the juice of 2 lemons. Pour into loaf pans and freeze. Keeps well for several days if frozen. Serve as a dessert in sherbet glasses, with a maraschino cherry, or in small bowls with toast or a sweet roll for a special breakfast.

VEGETABLES

BAKED POTATO

Before baking potatoes, cut them in half, insert a slice of onion, place sections together and bake as usual. Add a little butter and salt at the same time.

Select 1 medium-sized potato per person. Wash firmly using a stiff vegetable brush; cut away any softened or black spots. Wrap potatoes in foil and bake, or rub with shortening and put on rack, puncturing a few places with fork to prevent the skin breaking. Bake in 350° oven 1 hour. For an extra zip, crumble 3 or 4 slices crisp bacon into sour cream and serve with potatoes.

TWICE BAKED POTATOES

Select 1 large potato per serving (white potatoes preferred). Wash, wrap in foil, and bake 1 hour at 350°. Remove from oven, cut in half lengthwise, and carefully (hold with hot pad or several thicknesses of paper towel) scoop out the pulp of the potato. Do not break or tear shell. Mash potatoes, adding salt, milk, and butter while beating. Spoon mashed potato back into shells. Top with grated cheese, put in baking pan, cover with foil. Store in refrigerator until ½ hour before serving time. Put into 350° pre-heated oven, leaving them tightly covered. Serve piping hot. Leftovers, refrigerated, will be delicious reheated and served within a day or two.

FRENCH FRIED POTATOES

The more time you spend on your knees the less danger there is of falling.

Peel potatoes and cut into ½-inch strips lengthwise. Soak in cold water ½ hour. Drain thoroughly between paper towels. Heat fat to 350° or until a small piece of potato sizzles and comes to top of deep fat readily. Drop potatoes carefully into deep fat and cook until crisp and brown. Lift out and drain on paper towel. Sprinkle with salt and serve hot. (Care must be taken to dry potatoes well before dropping into fat, to avoid a bad burn.)

FRESH FRIED POTATOES

Peel potatoes and slice in medium thick slices. Fry in 2 tablespoons bacon drippings or other fat on low heat, tightly covered. Turn occasionally and fry until brown. Salt and pepper. Add slices of small onion if desired.

BUTTERED PARSLEY POTATOES

Scrub 4 medium-sized potatoes; cook with peeling on in salted water 30 minutes, or until tender. Cool slightly and remove peelings. (You can do this quickly in cold water and still keep them warm.)

While potatoes are cooking, melt two tablespoons butter over low heat. Add 2 tablespoons minced parsley and 1 teaspoon lemon juice. Roll potatoes in butter mixture until well coated. Serve at once. 2 to 4 servings.

BUTTER-CRUMB POTATOES

Prepare potatoes and cook as above. Roll in melted butter, then in finely rolled toasted bread crumbs. Place on cookie sheet and bake 15 to 20 minutes. Easy to prepare ahead of time as these need not be kept hot before rolling in butter and crumbs.

MASHED POTATOES FOR TWO

Peel 4 large potatoes and quarter. Boil, covered, 20 to 30 minutes until tender. Drain off liquid, and mash with potato masher or electric mixer, whipping until fluffy. Add ¼ to ½ cup milk, 1 tablespoon butter, 1 teaspoon salt; beat well. Serve hot.

Don't let anyone think little of you because you are young. Be their ideal; let them follow the way you teach and live; be a pattern for them in your love, your faith, and your clean thoughts.
1 TIMOTHY 4:12

QUICK SCALLOPED POTATOES

Melt butter in saucepan; stir in flour and salt. Add milk slowly and stir until mixture thickens. Add potatoes slowly and continue to stir until mixture boils again. Put in greased casserole and bake 35 minutes or until potatoes are done when tested with fork. Serves 5.

2 tablespoons butter
2 tablespoons flour
2 teaspoons salt
2 cups milk
6 cups raw sliced potatoes
(1 cup diced ham may be used to make a meat dish)

CANDIED SWEET POTATOES

Peel and cook 6 medium-sized sweet potatoes in salted water until tender, or use 1 large can sweet potatoes. Melt ½ cup butter or margarine in skillet. Add ⅓ cup brown sugar. Halve potatoes into skillet and cook over medium heat until coated a golden brown, turning several times. These may be prepared in the oven. Put cooked potatoes in baking dish, sprinkle with brown sugar, dot with butter. Bake 30 to 40 minutes in a 350° oven. Top with a few small marshmallows and brown in oven.

SCALLOPED SHREDDED POTATOES

Shred potatoes, dice onions fine, add salt. Place in baking dish. Pour hot white sauce over potatoes and stir. Dot with butter. Bake 45 minutes at 350°. Serves 4.

4 medium-sized potatoes, shredded
½ medium-sized onion, diced fine
½ teaspoon salt
1 recipe white sauce (p.112)

85

TABLE FOR COOKING VEGETABLES

Vegetable	Method	Cooking time		Liquid
		Frozen	Fresh	
Asparagus	Boiling	8-19 min.	10-20 min.	½ cup water
Green beans	Boiling	8-12 min.	15-30 min.	Cover vegetable
Navy beans (dry)	Boiling		3½-4 hrs.	Cover vegetable
Lima beans (dry)	Boiling		2-3 hrs.	Cover vegetable
Beets	Boiling		30-45 min.	Cover vegetable
Broccoli	Boiling	5-8 min.	15-20 min.	Small amount
Brussels sprouts	Boiling	6-8 min.	12-15 min.	Cover vegetable
Cabbage, quartered	Boiling		6-9 min.	Cover vegetable
Carrots, whole	Boiling		25-30 min.	Barely cover
Carrots, diced	Boiling	5-8 min.	20-30 min.	Barely cover
Cauliflower, divided	Boiling	5-8 min.	6-8 min.	Cover vegetable
Sweet corn (ear)*	Boiling	3 min.	4 min.	Generous amount
Corn kernels	Boiling	7-8 min.	4-5 min.	Cover vegetable
Eggplant (sliced)	French fry		2-3 min.	Hot oil
Mushrooms	Steam		4-5 min.	Cover vegetable
	Sauté		8-10 min.	2 tbsp. butter
Onions	Boiling		20-25 min.	Cover vegetable
Peas	Boiling	5-7 min.	12-20 min.	1 cup water
Potatoes	Boiling		30 min.	Cover vegetable
	Baking		45-60 min.	
	Steaming		30-45 min.	
Sweet potatoes	Boiling		20-30 min.	Small amount
	Baking		45-60 min.	
	Steaming		30-45 min.	
Rutabagas	Steaming		20-30 min.	Cover vegetable
Spinach	Steaming		8-10 min.	1 cup water
Squash (summer) sliced	Steaming		6-10 min.	1 cup water
Squash (winter)	Baked		60-70 min.	
Tomatoes	Stewing		5-7 min.	Small amount
	Baking		20-30 min.	
	Broiling		5-10 min.	
Turnips	Boiling		20-30 min.	Small amount
	Steaming		20-30 min.	Small amount

*Thaw before cooking.

Scrape or peel vegetables onto a paper towel; it takes just a moment to bundle it up and whisk into the garbage can.

Women should listen and learn quietly and humbly.
1 TIMOTHY 2:11

Use glycerin instead of oil to lubricate your beater or grinder and you will have no unpleasant taste in your food.

BROCCOLI

Wash broccoli thoroughly. Remove outer leaves; cut off tough portion of stalks; cut remaining stalk into 2-inch pieces. Cook covered in salted water until tender, 15 to 20 minutes. Drain. Serve buttered or with white sauce seasoned with grated cheese.

INDIAN CORN

Brown diced onions (and bacon if you are using this) in the fat. Add ham pieces, corn, milk, and potatoes. Season with salt and pepper. Cook (campfire outside is ideal) over low heat 25 to 30 minutes until potatoes are done. Stir frequently to prevent burning. Serves 6.

1 small onion, diced
2 tablespoons fat
1 cup cubed, cooked ham, or 8 slices crisp fried bacon
1 can cream-style corn
Milk
2 medium-sized potatoes, peeled and diced
Salt and pepper

CAULIFLOWER WITH CHEESE SAUCE

Remove leaves and cut flowerlets from woody base. Wash, cutting away any discolored places. Cook covered in boiling salted water for 8 to 10 minutes, or until tender. Drain and place in baking dish. Make one recipe white sauce (p. 114), folding in ¼ cup grated cheese. Pour sauce over cauliflower; top with buttered crumbs or crushed potato chips. Bake 30 minutes in 350° oven. Serves 4 to 6.

HARVARD BEETS

Mix cornstarch, sugar, salt, and pepper; add to butter, beet juice, and vinegar. Bring to boil over medium heat, stirring constantly. Add beets and bring to boil again. Serve hot. Makes 2 servings.

2 tablespoons butter
1 tablespoon cornstarch
2 teaspoons sugar
¼ teaspoon salt
Dash of pepper
⅓ cup beet juice
1½ teaspoons vinegar
1 8-ounce can cubed beets

CREAMED PEAS

Drain liquid from peas, add milk and butter. Mix flour and water in shaker (a small peanut butter jar with tight lid works fine for this). Combine ingredients and cook over low heat, stirring constantly. Season to taste with salt and pepper. Allow to boil and thicken. Remove from heat. Peas become mushy if overcooked.

2 cups cooked peas
1 cup milk
1 tablespoon butter
2 tablespoons flour
¼ cup water
Salt and pepper

CANDIED SQUASH

Peel thinly an acorn or hubbard squash. Cut in small pieces and place in buttered casserole. Top generously with brown sugar and ¼ cup butter. Bake 40 to 50 minutes in 350° oven. Cream may be used instead of butter.

BOSTON BAKED BEANS

1 pound navy beans, dry
2 medium onions, diced
½ cup molasses
¼ cup brown sugar,
  packed
1 teaspoon salt
1 teaspoon dry mustard
1 cup boiling water
¼ pound salt pork, cut
  in chunks

Wash beans, soak overnight, drain. Put beans in large saucepan; cover with water. Add diced onions and simmer for 1 hour or until tender. Drain. Turn into 2-quart casserole, adding 1 cup boiling water. Combine molasses, brown sugar, salt, and mustard and pour over beans. Place pork on top and bake at 300° for 6 hours. Add water to keep beans covered. Uncover for last ½ hour. Serves 6.

Meat, Poultry, and Fish

FOURTEEN

BUYING AND SELECTING MEATS

Meat is the most expensive single item in the food budget. It is also the highlight of most menus. Certain other foods just naturally "go" with a leg of lamb, a pork roast, or roast turkey. Because the larger part of a dollar is spent on meat, and because meat can make or break a meal, care should be used in selecting and preparing this most important food.

Every cut and grade of meat has an important place in the diet. The less expensive cuts, if cooked properly, can be just as tasty and certainly as nutritious as more expensive cuts.

Find a dependable store that carries the kind of meat that suits your taste in quality and price. It is important that you know the basic facts about meat.

The Federal Government provides inspection of meat by trained inspectors to prevent the sale of meat that is diseased or has been prepared under unsanitary conditions. The government also grades meat. There are seven official U.S. Government grades of beef but only four of these are commonly found in retail stores.

USDA Choice is preferred by most consumers because it is of high quality and has little fat. Roasts and steaks from the loin and ribs are tender and juicy. More suitable for pot roasts are the cuts from the round or chuck, but they may also be dry roasted.

USDA Good is a more thrifty grade and has other desirable qualities. It has little fat and is not quite as juicy as the Choice grade of beef.

USDA Standard is produced largely from older animals and is not as tender as Choice or Good. If it is cooked longer and more slowly, very satisfactory results can be obtained.

USDA Commercial grade beef is produced mostly from older cattle. It is not juicy and is not so tender. But again, it provides lean meats for stews, ground meat dishes, and pot roasts.

Veal and calf are graded in the same way.

Use baking soda as a cleanser to restore the transparency of your glass oven door.

89

Pork produced in the United States is generally more standard than other meat, minimizing the need fo grading.

There are two basic ways of cooking meats: either dry heat (roasting, broiling, frying, or barbecuing) or moist heat (braising, stewing, or simmering). The method to be used depends on the cut and the grade of meat. Dry heat cooking is most successful with meats that are generously covered with fat and which become tender quickly when cooked. Moist heat is used for the grades of meat which are not so tender and require longer, slower cooking.

Use your roast four ways. First as a roast; second in hot beef sandwiches (using leftover gravy); third in French dip sandwiches; fourth, in stew. Boil stew vegetables until done. Drop in cubed beef and bouillon. Cook an additional 15 minutes.

Sprinkle a liberal amount of baking soda or salt to extinguish a grease fire on the stove.

PAN-FRIED BACON
Put sliced bacon in skillet over low heat. As bacon warms, gently separate slices and lay flat in pan. Turn bacon several times while cooking until crisp. Drain on paper toweling.

BROILED BACON
Separate slices. (Leave bacon out of refrigerator ½ hour so it will separate without tearing.) Place slices on broiler rack 3 inches from heat. When brown on one side, turn to brown other side.

BAKED BACON
Heat oven to 375°. Place separated slices on rack which fits into larger pan or on cookie sheet with sides to catch fat. Bake 10 to 15 minutes until crisp and brown. You need not turn it.

BACON DRIPPINGS
Whether frying, broiling, or baking, save the grease by pouring, when slightly cool, into metal or ceramic container. (Glass or plastic may crack and you may receive a severe burn.) Bacon grease adds flavor when frying eggs, potatoes, omelets, French toast, etc.; may be used as shortening in pancakes and waffles. Keep refrigerated.

CANADIAN BACON
Place slices in cold skillet. Heat slowly; turn slices to brown evenly on each side.

PAN-FRIED SAUSAGES
Put sausages in cold skillet over low heat and cook until evenly browned, turning often. Depending on the size of sausages used, cook from 10 to 16 minutes. Serve hot with eggs, griddle cakes, or waffles.

If bulk sausage (purchased like hamburger) is used, make rather small patties, brown in skillet on both sides, cover and cook over low heat 15 to 20 minutes. Be sure the sausage is thoroughly cooked. Pork must always be well done with no pink color.

POT ROAST DINNER

Flour and salt meat; brown in small amount of fat. Add water, cover, cook slowly until tender, 2 to 3 hours. When meat is nearly tender (about 40 minutes before serving time) add all vegetables except cabbage and cook 30 minutes. Add cabbage, season all vegetables with salt, and cook 10 minutes. Add water as necessary during cooking time; do not let it cook dry. Serves 6.

3 pounds beef roast (rump or heel of round)
½ cup water
6 carrots
6 potatoes
3 small onions
½ head cabbage, cut in thirds

MEAT LOAF

Mix together first eight ingredients. In a separate bowl combine bread, milk, eggs, and Worcestershire sauce. Mix thoroughly with meat mixture and shape into loaf. Bake in shallow oblong pan in 350° oven 1 hour. Pour 1 can tomato sauce over loaf and bake additional 30 minutes. Serves 6.

1½ pounds ground beef
½ pound ground pork
⅓ cup chopped onion
2 tablespoons chopped celery
2 teaspoons salt
¼ teaspoon pepper
¼ teaspoon dry mustard
½ teaspoon poultry seasoning
4 slices soft bread, crumbed
1 cup warm milk
2 eggs
1 tablespoon Worcestershire sauce

INDIVIDUAL MEAT LOAVES—JUST FOR TWO

Combine beef, pork, seasonings, and eggs. Mix well; add bread crumbs and milk. Add more milk if mixture seems too thick. Divide into 2 loaves and wrap each with a slice of bacon. Secure bacon with toothpick. Broil 25 to 30 minutes, 4 inches from heat.

½ pound ground beef
¼ pound ground pork
½ teaspoon salt
Dash pepper
1 beaten egg
⅓ cup fine bread crumbs
3 tablespoons milk
2 slices bacon
2 tablespoons chopped onion

FRANK BOATS

Cut a slit in each frank lengthwise, being careful not to cut completely through. Put ½-inch strips of American cheese into slits. Place in baking dish. For each pound of frankfurters, prepare one recipe of the sauce (at right). Mix all ingredients well. Pour sauce over franks and bake in 350° oven 20 minutes. Sauce may be prepared and kept refrigerated.

⅓ cup pickle relish
½ cup catsup
1 tablespoon Worcestershire sauce
½ teaspoon dry mustard
¼ cup hot water
¼ teaspoon salt

OVEN BARBECUED CHICKEN

Cut 1 chicken into serving-size pieces. Brown in 2 tablespoons fat. Place in baking dish and cover with Hot Sauce (p. 113). Bake 1 to 1½ hours in 350° oven.

When dredging or coating meat, put the flour on a piece of clean newspaper, paper towel, or paper plate, which can be thrown away after use.

BROILED FRANKS
Slit frankfurters lengthwise, but not clear through. Fill slit with wedges of processed cheese. Wrap each frankfurter in one slice bacon, securing with toothpick. Place under broiler slit side down and broil until bacon is crisp. Turn carefully with tongs or two forks and broil until other side of bacon is crisp.

FRIED HALIBUT
Salt and pepper two medium-sized halibut slices; roll in flour. Pan fry in 3 tablespoons hot fat in heavy skillet until golden brown. Carefully turn with a spatula and brown other side. If slices are unusually thick add 2 tablespoons water, cover, and steam for an additional 3 to 4 minutes to be sure fish is well done. Serve hot with lemon slices and tartar sauce.

QUICK TARTAR SAUCE
Mix all ingredients well.

½ cup salad dressing
1 teaspoon finely chopped onion
2 tablespoons finely chopped dill pickle
2 tablespoons milk

SALMON SUPPER
Brown onion and green pepper in fat; stir in salt and flour. Gradually add soup and milk, stirring constantly. Bring to boil and boil 1 minute. Add salmon, peas, and lemon juice. Pour into greased oblong baking dish. Top with biscuits (p. 57) and bake 12 to 15 minutes in 400° oven. (Use half of biscuit recipe, or 1 package prepared biscuits.)

3 tablespoons onion, diced fine
⅓ cup green pepper, diced fine
3 tablespoons fat
½ teaspoon salt
1 can cream of celery soup (or mushroom soup)
1½ cups milk
1 7-ounce can salmon, drained
1 cup peas, cooked
¼ cup flour
1 teaspoon lemon juice

BEEF STEW
Dredge meat cubes in flour, salt, and pepper; brown in hot fat on all sides. Remove pan from heat and slowly add water. Bring to low boil over medium heat. Simmer 2 hours, adding additional water if needed. Add celery, onions, and carrots and cook 15 minutes. Add potatoes and soup and cook 30 minutes longer or until vegetables are tender. Here is an easy, complete meal in one dish.

1 pound beef cubes for stewing
2 tablespoons flour
1 teaspoon salt
¼ teaspoon pepper
1 quart hot water
1 large onion, quartered
4 medium-sized potatoes, quartered
4 medium-sized carrots, cut in chunks
1 stalk celery
1 can cream of tomato soup

BROILED STEAK

Select a T-bone, sirloin, tenderloin, or club steak cut 1 to 2 inches thick. Preheat broiler or cook on grill over whitened coals. Place meat 2 to 3 inches from heat. Broil on one side, turn and broil on the other. Season and serve immediately.

   1-inch steaks, 15 to 20 minutes cooking time
   1½-inch steaks, 25 minutes
   2-inch steaks, 30 to 35 minutes

Before broiling meat, cut the edges at one-inch intervals with a sharp knife to prevent the meat from curling up.

BAKED STEAK

Cut meat into serving size pieces. Dip into eggs thoroughly, coat with cracker crumbs. Brown quickly in fat and place in shallow 9" x 13" baking dish. Make gravy as directed on package, or make a thin water gravy mixing 1 tablespoon flour and 1 cup water in skillet. Pour gravy over meat, cover pan tightly with foil and bake 1 hour in 300° oven. Put thick slices of onion on steaks before covering and baking if desired. Serves 6.

1 to 2 pounds round
   steak
1 well-beaten egg
2 tablespoons milk
1 cup fine cracker
   crumbs
2 tablespoons fat
Salt and pepper
1 package prepared
   gravy mix

CHICKEN-FRIED STEAK

Prepare meat as in Baked Steak. Fry over medium heat in 4 table-spoons fat. Brown one side, turn and brown other. Season. Cover and turn heat very low. Cook 45 minutes, if necessary adding tiny bit of water to keep from burning. (Cube steaks work fine and are often less expensive than other kinds of steak.)

FRIED CHICKEN

Melt 2 or 3 rounded tablespoons shortening in heavy skillet. Wash and clean frying chicken; cut into serving pieces. Put ¾ cup flour, 1 tablespoon salt, ¼ teaspoon pepper, and 1 teaspoon paprika into a medium-sized brown paper bag. Dredge the chicken in the flour mixture two or three pieces at a time, shaking the bag until the pieces are well coated. Put chicken in skillet; cover tightly. Brown on both sides in fairly hot skillet, 360° if using electric skillet. When chicken is browned on all sides reduce heat to 260° (low) and continue frying about 50 minutes or until tender. The amount of time will depend upon the size of the chicken.

To coat chicken for frying, put ½ to 1 cup of flour into a medium-sized paper bag, fold top over, and shake. This distributes the flour evenly. Use the flour that is left in the bag to thicken gravy.

STUFFED PORK CHOPS

Allow 2 pork chops for each serving. Flour chops and place in shallow pan. Crumble 6 or 8 slices of bread into a bowl; add 1 teaspoon poultry seasoning and 1 teaspoon salt. Pour boiling water over mixture just to moisten. Cover each chop with an inch of stuffing, top with second chop and bake in 375° oven 1 hour. Diced onion adds to the flavor of the stuffing.

BREADED PORK CHOPS

1 or 2 chops per serving, depending on size
1 egg
3 tablespoons milk
½ cup finely rolled cracker crumbs

Break egg into small bowl and beat with fork until well mixed; add milk. Dip pork chop into egg mixture, then roll in cracker crumbs. Pan fry in 3 tablespoons fat, slowly browning each side. If chops are unusually large or thick, turn heat down after browning and add 2 tablespoons water. Cover tightly and steam an additional 5 to 7 minutes to be sure the pork is thoroughly cooked.

PORK CHOPS SUPREME

Put 1 medium-sized pork chop or two small chops per person in bottom of shallow pan. Pour in 1 can tomato soup. Sprinkle dried celery leaves generously over soup. Bake in 350° oven 1 hour, uncovered. Very good when served with potatoes baked in the oven at the same time.

PAN-FRIED HAM

Don't praise yourself; let others do it!
PROVERBS 27:2

Slice ham to desired thickness, then cut fat edges with sharp knife. Melt 1 tablespoon shortening in heavy skillet over high heat. Lay ham slices in skillet, brown quickly on each side. Any kind of boiled or baked ham may be cooked this way and makes tasty hot sandwiches. Ham that is uncooked must be fried a little longer using lower heat, 5 to 7 minutes for each side.

SAUSAGE RING

2 pounds ground pork sausage (not links)
2 eggs
2 tablespoons grated onion
1½ cups fine bread crumbs
¼ cup parsley, if desired

Preheat oven to 350°. Generously butter a metal ring mold. Mix ingredients well and pack into mold with the back of a spoon. Bake 20 minutes, remove from oven and pour extra fat carefully into a metal or ceramic container (hot fat will break glass). Bake 20 minutes more, turn out onto platter and fill center with scrambled or creamed eggs.

ROAST CHICKEN AND DRESSING

Select dressed roasting chicken allowing ½ pound per serving. If frozen, leave wrapping on and set in kitchen sink overnight to thaw. (You may hurry thawing by placing in deep pan and covering with warm water.) Remove giblets from neck or inside cavity and cook in salted water 1 hour. Wash and clean chicken thoroughly; pat dry with paper towel. Sprinkle inside with salt. Stuff *loosely,* using 1 cup dressing per pound of chicken. Close opening with toothpicks or metal roasting pins. Tie legs together with a strong string; fold wing tips across back. Rub skin gently with shortening. Place in roaster pan breast side up. Do not add water. Cover with roaster lid or large sheet of aluminum foil. Bake at 350° 30 minutes per pound for chicken 3½ pounds or less; 25 minutes per pound for over 4 pounds.

FRIED LIVER AND ONIONS

Dip liver slices in flour and brown on each side in 2 tablespoons fat. Season; add 2 more tablespoons fat. Add 1 to 2 cups sliced onions and cover tightly. Cook over moderate heat, stirring every 5 minutes. Continue frying until onions are tender. Use the fat in the skillet after frying liver and onions to make gravy as usual.

GRANDMA'S BREAD STUFFING

Combine bread cubes, melted margarine, finely cut cooked giblet pieces, onions, celery, and seasonings; mix well. Add cooled giblet liquid and cold water to thoroughly moisten crumbs. Stuff bird. Extra dressing may be baked by spooning into the pan next to the fowl to absorb some of the drippings and be more tasty than if baked separately. Remove from pan just before making gravy. Don't be too careful to remove every bit of dressing; it will flavor the gravy.

4 cups dry bread, cubed
⅓ cup margarine, melted
1 small onion
¼ cup celery, diced fine
Sage to taste, 2 to 4 tablespoons
Salt and pepper
Cooked giblets and liquid

CREAMED CHICKEN OR TURKEY

Select a 3 to 4 pound stewing chicken (or a small roasting turkey). Wash and clean thoroughly and cut into pieces. Place in large pan and barely cover with water. Add 1 teaspoon salt. Bring to boil, then turn to simmer, and slowly cook until the meat falls from the bone. Add more water as needed. Remove pan from stove, lift meat pieces onto platter to cool, pick off meat from the bones, and cut into smaller chunks. From a medium-sized chicken there will be 1 to 1½ quarts stock. If not, add enough milk to make 1½ quarts liquid. Mix 4 rounded tablespoons flour with ¾ cup cold water and stir until smooth. Heat the broth and the chicken pieces together to a low boil, then add flour mixture gradually, stirring constantly to prevent lumping. Salt and pepper to taste and serve on hot biscuits, mashed potatoes, or toast. This may be cooked the day before, refrigerated overnight, then heated as above. An economical way to prepare this dish is to save the bony pieces from frying chicken, freeze them until of sufficient quantity, boil, thicken the broth and meat, and you have a no-left-over leftover. If cooking for two, prepare a whole chicken, freeze half of the cooked broth and chicken, and bring it out next week!

Trust in the Lord God always, for in the Lord Jehovah is your everlasting strength.

ISAIAH 26:4

CREAMY PERCH BAKE

Place fish in casserole. Mix soup, sour cream, and onions. Spoon over fish. Bake for 30 minutes at 350°. Arrange Tater Tots around the fish and bake 30 minutes more.
Note: Or you can use a package of dehydrated scalloped potatoes prepared according to package directions. Spoon around the fish and bake 15 to 30 minutes more.

1 pound fish fillets (deboned)
1 can cream of shrimp soup
½ cup sour cream
2 tablespoons chopped onions
1 package Tater Tots

PAT'S BEEF STEW

1 4-pound beef roast
1 onion
4 potatoes
8 carrots
1 can beef consommé
    soup
1 16-ounce can
    tomatoes
3 tablespoons minute
    tapioca

Cut the meat into small pieces, about 1½ inch cubes. Cut up onion, potatoes, and carrots. Combine remaining ingredients and place in roaster. Cover and bake at 250° for 5 hours.

CORDON BLEU

4 chicken breasts
4 thin ham slices
2 ounces Swiss cheese
Flour
1 egg
½ cup milk
2 cups bread crumbs or
    cracker crumbs

Skin and bone chicken breasts. Flatten with the heel of your hand. Wrap a slice of ham around a piece of cheese about 2″ long and ¼″ wide. Then wrap the chicken breast around the ham and cheese. You may want to use a toothpick to secure it. Then dip the breasts in flour and then in an egg wash (the beaten egg in about ½ cup milk) and then in finely crushed cracker crumbs. Brown in hot oil about 4 minutes to a side. You may want to finish your Cordon Bleu in your microwave. Just place them on a platter and set in your oven on roast or medium setting for about 1½ minutes. This will assure their being piping hot when you serve them.

MAGNIFICENT CHICKEN

6 chicken breasts
½ cup melted margarine
1 egg
½ cup milk
2 teaspoons lemon
    pepper
1 3-ounce package
    cream cheese
½ cup milk
1 can cream of
    mushroom soup
1 medium size can
    mushrooms
4 green onions

Skin chicken breasts. Dip in melted margarine, then in the egg, beaten into ½ cup milk and seasoned with 1 teaspoon lemon pepper. Place on a rack in your oven at 350° and bake for 30 minutes.

While the chicken is baking, prepare the sauce. Combine cream cheese, milk, juice from the mushrooms, and the soup. A blender works very well for this. When smooth, add the mushrooms and chopped green onions and season with 1 teaspoon lemon pepper. Remove chicken from oven and place in a 9″ x 13″ baking dish—or one large enough to hold the chicken. Top with the sauce and bake at 250° for 2½ hours.

BARBECUED BRISKET ROAST

Sauce
2 cups ketchup
1 cup water
2 teaspoons lemon juice
⅓ cup Worcestershire
    sauce
1 teaspoon chili powder
1 teaspoon salt
½ cup plus 2
    tablespoons brown
    sugar
1 medium onion, grated
3 teaspoons liquid smoke
A dash of Tabasco sauce

Rub ½ teaspoon ginger and ½ teaspoon dry mustard into brisket. Bake uncovered 3 to 4 hours. Let cool 1 hour. Slice thin across the grain of the beef. Pour off fat.

Mix all ingredients for sauce well. Pour sauce over meat and bake 3 hours at 300° in a well-covered pan.

BARBECUED RIBS

Sprinkle spare ribs with salt and pepper. May add 2 tablespoons of lemon juice or lemon slices if desired. Bake uncovered 45 minutes at 450°. Add hickory flavored barbecue sauce. Remove lemon slices if used. Bake uncovered 3 more hours at 200°.

ROASTING CHART FOR MEAT AND POULTRY

	Weight	Temp.		Minutes Per Lb.
BEEF				
Standing rib	6 to 8 pounds	300°	rare	18 to 20
		300°	medium	22 to 25
		300°	well	27 to 30
Rolled rib	6 to 8 pounds	300°	rare	32
		300°	medium	38
		300°	well	48
Chuck roast	6 to 8 pounds	300°	well	30
Rump roast	5 to 7 pounds	300°	well	30
LAMB				
Leg or shoulder	5½ to 7½ pounds	300°		30
Shoulder, rolled	3 to 4 pounds	300°		45
POULTRY				
Chicken and duck	4 to 6 pounds	350°		30 to 35
Goose	10 to 12 pounds	325°		20 to 25
Turkey	8 to 10 pounds	325°		20 to 25
	10 to 14 pounds	325°		18 to 20
	14 to 18 pounds	300°		15 to 18
PORK—FRESH				
Loin center	3 to 4 pounds	350°		40
Loin whole	12 to 15 pounds	350°		20
Loin end	3 to 4 pounds	350°		50
Shoulder	12 to 14 pounds	350°		35
Boned and rolled	4 to 6 pounds	350°		45
Pork butt	4 to 6 pounds	350°		50
PORK—SMOKED				
Ham—whole	10 to 12 pounds	300°		25
Ham—new type	10 to 12 pounds	300°		15
Ham—half	6 pounds	300°		30
Ham—new type	6 pounds	300°		20
Ham—shank end	3 pounds	300°		40
Ham—butt end	3 pounds	300°		45
VEAL				
Leg roast	7 to 8 pounds	300°		25
Loin	4½ to 5 pounds	300°		35
Shoulder	7 pounds	300°		25
Shoulder—rolled	5 pounds	300°		45

To line a pan with foil in a hurry, turn pan upside-down, press foil smoothly to the out-side of the pan, lift foil and turn pan over. The foil drops in easily and fits smoothly.

GRAVY

There are two ways to make gravy in the skillet in which the meat cooked. One way is to remove all but 2 tablespoons fat from the pan, or add a little fat if needed. Add 2 tablespoons flour and stir well, scraping the crusty particles from the pan into the flour and fat. Stir until brown. Turn heat down and add liquid, either milk or water, stirring constantly. Potato water adds flavor. Keep heat low, or gravy will become lumpy as liquid is added. Pour in about 1 cup liquid, stir well; add more liquid gradually, stirring constantly, until gravy reaches desired consistency. Salt and pepper.

The other way is to add the desired amount of milk or water to the drippings. Keep heat low so liquid doesn't steam up when added to the fat. In a jar with a tight lid, combine 3 tablespoons flour with 1 cup cold water, screw lid on tight, and shake well. Add flour-water a little at a time to hot liquid, stirring constantly to prevent lumpy gravy. Milk is generally used with fowl or steak to make gravy, while water is preferred with ham and other pork. However, the liquid used and the thickness of the gravy are according to preference. Salt and pepper before serving.

GRAVY FROM BAKED FOWL

Remove fowl and dressing from roaster pan, covering with foil to keep warm while making gravy. Place roaster pan over low heat. Add 2 cups milk to drippings and stir until milk is steaming hot. Make a flour and water paste. Pour a little at a time into pan, stirring constantly until gravy is as thick as desired. Salt to taste.

Save a small peanut butter or mayonnaise jar with a lid to use for mixing flour and water for making gravy. Put water in the jar first and then add the flour and it is less likely to be lumpy. Shake vigorously. These jars may be used to store leftovers. You can see what is in them and be less likely to waste the food.

Microwave Cooking

FIFTEEN

MICROWAVE HINTS

- Do not use newsprint in any form in your microwave as toxic fumes are produced in heating.
- Styrofoam can be used in heating a few seconds, but it also produces toxic gases on high heat.
- Paper towels, plates, etc., are safe for short time use, but glassware, ceramics, or microwave dishes are safer for high or longer heating.
- Cover food that may splatter, using waxed paper as it steams and becomes moist. Paper towels or napkins may get soggy if used for that purpose.
- If fire *should* break out in your microwave turn the control to off and cover the vent with a cloth towel to cut off the oxygen supply. Do not open the door until the fire is out.
- Read your microwave oven instructions concerning the use of aluminum foil. Some say it is safe and others advise against using it.
- Do not heat food in glass jars with an opening smaller than the jar. Use open dishes or bowls. Baby food jars may pop. When heating baby food be careful not to heat too long. Remember that food continues to cook after the microwave is turned off.
- Use only sturdy paper plates to hold food or place light weight paper plates on micro-safe plates or glass pie dishes.
- Puddings and white sauces cook very well in microwave ovens. Just remember to stir every 30 to 45 seconds. No more burned pans in cooking milk.
- Microwaving time is always directly related to the amount of food you are cooking. The more food, the longer the cooking time. A little experimenting will soon give you the amount of time necessary for the quantities you usually prepare.
- To reheat vegetables without adding much water, wet the inside of the lid of the dish you are using.
- To soften butter or margarine after being in the freezer, unwrap and place on butter dish and microwave 15 seconds on low heat for refrigerated butter and 30 seconds for frozen.

- Make your own bread cubes for stuffing by cubing the bread. Place it in an 8" x 12" dish and microwave 6 to 7 minutes, stirring each minute.
- Shelling nuts is easy in the microwave. For 2 cups of nuts add 1 cup of water and place in a 1 quart bowl. Cook 4 to 5 minutes. Nuts come out easily when cracked.
- Raisins and other dried fruit which have hardened can be softened in your microwave. Sprinkle 1 or 2 teaspoons of water on a package of raisins or dried fruit which have been placed in a micro-wave-proof bowl. Cover and microwave 45 to 50 seconds.
- Re-crisp stale potato chips, corn chips, etc. by microwaving 4 to 5 seconds. Let stand a few minutes before serving.
- Any bakery goods can be refreshed by microwaving a few seconds.
- *Never* operate your microwave oven if the door does not close tightly or if it becomes bent, warped, or damaged. Unless the door is properly in place the microwave may give off harmful radiation.
- Clean your microwave oven carefully including the doors and seal using water and a mild detergent. *Do not* use scouring pads, abrasive cleaners, or steel wool. Usually a stubborn spot will come clean easily if you place a wet dishcloth on it and leave it for an hour or so.
- *Do not* turn on an empty oven.
- Add salt after cooking.
- Do not cook vegetables in boilable pouch without first making a slash to let the steam out.
- Seal juices in meat and chicken for barbecuing by microwaving for 15 to 20 minutes while the briquets are starting. Then baste with barbecue sauce and finish cooking on the grill.

MICROWAVE RECIPES
Appetizers

BACON FLOWERS
Layer bacon between paper towels and microwave on high for ½ minute per slice. When cool enough to handle, roll and stick on end of a toothpick. Cut green olives in half and slide onto toothpick as leaves. Use a square of mild cheese for a base.

BACON STIX

10 thin bread sticks
10 slices bacon
½ cup grated parmesan
   cheese

Cover one side of uncooked bacon with parmesan cheese. Lay bread stick on strip diagonally and wrap with bacon. Place strips on micro-baking sheet lined with paper towels. Microwave on high 4½ to 6 minutes. Roll again in cheese. When cool, stand in glass to serve.

NACHOS

Spread tortilla chips on a paper plate. Sprinkle with shredded mild cheese. Dot with taco sauce. Microwave on 50% for 1½ to 2 minutes.

COCKTAIL WIENERS

Combine sauce and seasonings in a 1½ quart covered casserole. Microwave on high 1½ to 2½ minutes until bubbling. Stir in wieners and cover. Microwave 4 to 6 minutes, stirring once. Serve with cocktail picks.

1 pound wieners or cocktail sausages
1½ cups barbecue sauce
2 tablespoons brown sugar
⅛ teaspoon dry mustard
½ teaspoon ginger

HAM ROLL-UPS

Cook broccoli spears 8 minutes or until tender. Lay 1 slice American cheese on one slice of cooked ham. Lay 1 broccoli spear on cheese, then roll and place in a baking dish. Pour canned mushroom soup over rolled ham. Fresh mushrooms may be added. Use as many slices of cheese and ham as you need, plus enough broccoli to fill the roll-ups. Bake on high 1 to 2 minutes per roll-up until they are heated through.

MEXICAN TACO DIP

Salt and pepper, then brown hamburger. Dice onions and green peppers and stir into hamburger. Add refried beans and green chilies. Place on baking dish. Sprinkle shredded cheese on top, then drizzle taco sauce over all. Cover and chill until time to bake. Bake 20 minutes or until bubbly in microwave. Good served with sour cream or guacamole on top.

1 pound hamburger
¼ green pepper
¾ cup mild taco sauce
1 small onion, diced
1 can refried beans if desired
½ pound cheddar cheese
1 4-ounce can green chilies if desired

Candy

PEANUT BRITTLE

Combine syrup, sugar, and salt in a 2-quart casserole or mixing bowl. Microwave on high for 5 minutes. Stir in peanuts and microwave 5 minutes, stirring once at 3 minutes. Stir in butter, vanilla, and baking soda and beat until light and foamy. Spread as thin as possible onto a greased cookie sheet. Cool and break in pieces.

½ cup light corn syrup
1 cup sugar
⅛ teaspoon salt
1½ cups salted peanuts
1 tablespoon butter
1 teaspoon vanilla
1 teaspoon baking soda

BAVARIAN MINTS by Jan

Melt first 3 ingredients for 2 minutes on high, stirring every 20 or 30 seconds. Stir until smooth. Remove from microwave and add condensed milk, vanilla, and peppermint. Beat on low speed for 1 minutes and on high speed 2 minutes. Pour into 8-inch square buttered pan. Refrigerate.

3 cups milk chocolate chips (1½ bags)
1 square unsweetened chocolate
1 tablespoon butter
1 can Eagle Brand sweetened condensed milk
1 teaspoon vanilla
1 teaspoon peppermint extract

Desserts

BAKED APPLES

Core apples. Mix together 1 tablespoon brown sugar and ½ table-spoon butter for every apple used. Place butter and sugar in core holes. Arrange in baking dish with space between apples. Cover tightly.

Microwave on high 2½ to 4½ minutes for every 2 apples or until tender. I usually use 4 to 6 minutes for 4 apples. Rotate after 2 minutes or until the apples are fork-tender. Allow to stand 2 minutes before serving.

APPLE CRISP

6 apples
1 tablespoon lemon
    juice
¾ cup brown sugar
¾ cup quick-cook
    oatmeal
½ cup flour
1 teaspoon cinnamon
6 tablespoons margarine

Peel, core, and slice apples. Place in 8-inch square dish. Sprinkle with lemon juice. Melt margarine in small mixing bowl on high in microwave oven for 1 to 1½ minutes. Add remaining ingredients and stir until crumbly. Sprinkle over apples evenly. Press down lightly. Microwave on high 8 minutes. Rotate a half turn and microwave another 6 to 8 minutes or until apples are tender.

Sauces

REFRIGERATOR WHITE SAUCE

¼ cup butter or
    margarine
¼ cup flour
2 cups chicken broth
    (canned & undiluted)
½ cup whipping cream
½ teaspoon salt
¼ teaspoon pepper
¼ cup parmesan cheese

Melt butter in large glass measuring cup for 30 seconds on high. Stir in flour until smooth. Gradually add broth, blending thoroughly. Microwave for 5 minutes stirring every 60 seconds. Add cream, salt, and pepper. Add parmesan cheese.

This is good poured over fried or baked chicken. Garnish with paprika. It is also good as a base in creamed soups, such as cauliflower or asparagus.

JAN'S WHITE SAUCE

½ cup melted butter
1½ cups dry milk
¾ cup flour
½ teaspoon dry mustard
½ teaspoon salt
¼ cup water

Mix first three ingredients. Add remaining ingredients and mix well. Dough will be stiff. Turn mixture onto wax paper, making into a 1-foot long roll. Wrap roll in wax paper. Store in refrigerator. For ½ cup sauce, cut a 1-inch slice off roll and mix well with ½ cup of water. Heat in microwave as needed.

Salads and Dressings

SIXTEEN

SALADS

ORANGE CREME JELL-O SALAD

Dissolve Jell-O in boiling water. Add frozen orange sherbet immediately, stirring until sherbet is dissolved. Add remaining liquid. Stir and chill until partially set. Whip cream and fold into Jell-O. Fold in mandarin oranges and pour into mold. Chill until firm.

2 3-ounce packages
   orange Jell-O
1½ cups boiling water
1 pint orange sherbet
1 small can mandarin
   oranges, drained
Juice of oranges and
   water to make 1 cup
½ pint whipping crear

MOCK CHICKEN SALAD

Dissolve Jell-O in hot water. Chill until nearly firm. Add tuna, olives, and celery; fold in mayonnaise. Chill. Serve with hot rolls and butter.

   To unmold Jell-O salad, fill pan larger than mold pan with hot water. Immerse Jell-O mold in pan of hot water 2 to 3 seconds. Remove, place salad plate upside down over Jell-O mold and turn quickly. Jell-O should fall out easily onto center of plate. Chill until serving time.

1 3-ounce package
   lemon Jell-O
1½ cups hot water
1 can flaked tuna
½ cup sliced olives
1 cup chopped celery
½ cup mayonnaise

WHIPPED GELATIN FREEZE

Prepare two 3-ounce packages any flavor of gelatin following package directions. Freeze in 1-quart refrigerator tray. Break in small chunks and beat with electric mixer until very smooth. Serve at once. Serves 6.

PINEAPPLE SUNBURST SALAD

Combine 1 3-ounce package orange Jell-O with 1¾ cups boiling water; stir to dissolve. Add 1 cup crushed pineapple, drained, and 2 or 4 grated fresh carrots. Chill, cut in squares, and serve.

PINEAPPLE-CHEESE RINGAROUND

For each individual salad you will need 1 ring of sliced pineapple placed on a leaf of lettuce. Spoon a mound of cottage cheese on center and sprinkle with grated cheddar cheese. Quick, easy, and good!

CHEESE MACARONI SALAD

2 cups cooked macaroni
1 cup diced celery
1 cup cooked peas
¼ cup shredded raw
 carrots
1 green pepper,
 shredded
Salt and pepper
Mayonnaise

Mix all ingredients well, garnish with cheese balls or sliced stuffed olives.

BUTTERFLY BANANA SALAD

Split bananas in half lengthwise, then in half in the middle. Place two sections on a lettuce leaf to form butterfly wings. Add mayonnaise thinned with a bit of cream to form the body. Sprinkle with chopped nuts. Quick, pretty, and delicious!

FRUIT PLATE

Prayer is the key to heaven, and faith unlocks the door.

Combine available fresh fruits with canned fruits and arrange either on individual salad plates or one large plate for the table. Canned pear halves, sliced peaches, or mandarin oranges are nice. Quartered apples, banana slices, grapes, fresh or canned pineapple slices are tasty. Add color with a few maraschino cherries. For lunch, add a scoop of sherbet and serve with hot rolls, butter, and jelly.

LIME JELL-O PEAR SALAD

Mix 2 3-ounce packages of lime Jell-O as directed on package, using liquid from 1 large can pear halves as part of liquid. Arrange pear halves in bottom of ring mold. Pour Jell-O in to barely cover pears and place in refrigerator to chill. When firm, add remaining Jell-O and return to chill. Unmold and serve with grated cheese. Refreshing!

TOMATO ASPIC

1 3-ounce package
 lemon Jell-O
1¼ cups hot water
1 can tomato sauce
1 tablespoon vinegar

Dissolve Jell-O in hot water. Add tomato sauce and vinegar. Pour into mold and chill. This is excellent with meat dishes.

CHEF'S SALAD

1 clove garlic
½ head lettuce (or
 romaine)
1 cup cooked ham strips
1 slice swiss cheese
¼ cup chopped green
 onion
¼ cup diced celery
1 flat can anchovy if desired
1 hard-cooked egg
4 ripe olives

Rub salad bowl with cut garlic clove. Tear lettuce into bite-sized pieces and line bowl. Toss in remaining greens, onions, and celery. Arrange ham and cheese on lettuce. Lay egg slices, ripe olives, and anchovies on top. Serve in individual salad bowls and pass assorted salad dressings to meet each person's taste.

POTATO SALAD

Dice potatoes, add other ingredients, and stir well. If salad seems dry, add a few teaspoons milk or cream to moisten. Garnish with sliced hardcooked egg, sliced olive, or parsley. Serves 6.

4 to 6 cooked potatoes
4 hard-cooked eggs, diced
1 small onion, diced fine
¾ cup salad dressing
1 teaspoon prepared
   mustard
Diced celery and
   cucumbers if desired
Salt and pepper

RED HOT APPLESAUCE SALAD

Melt ⅓ cup red-hot candies in ½ cup boiling water. Combine 3 3-ounce boxes cherry Jell-O, 3 cups boiling water, and stir to dissolve. Cool 10 minutes. Add 3 cups applesauce and red-hot mixture to Jell-O. Stir and pour into 11″ x 13″ pan. Chill in refrigerator until firm. Combine 2 3-ounce packages cream cheese, ½ cup cream, whipped, and ½ cup mayonnaise and spread over Jell-O. This cuts better if made a day ahead. Serves 12.

RED KIDNEY BEAN SALAD

Mix ingredients, carefully folding mayonnaise in last. Chill well and serve on lettuce leaf.

1 can red kidney beans,
   drained
1 small onion, diced fine
¼ cup celery, chopped
   fine
2 hard-cooked eggs,
   diced
½ teaspoon salt
Dash pepper
¼ to ⅓ cup mayonnaise

TOSSED SALAD

Prepare salad greens ahead of time by washing, draining, and drying them. Chill in a ventilated bowl in refrigerator. At serving time *tear* leaf or head lettuce into bite-sized pieces. If you enjoy garlic, rub inside of salad bowl with cut clove of garlic, then throw the garlic away. Use almost any fresh vegetable: tomatoes, sliced and quartered, cucumber slices or cubes, finely cut green onions, sliced radishes, thinly sliced or shredded carrots, small pieces of cauliflower, celery chopped fine. Add shredded or cubed cheese, diced hard-cooked eggs, and chopped pickles and olives, if desired. Add favorite dressing and toss lightly to distribute vegetables and dressing.

Do you want to be truly rich? You already are if you are happy and good.

1 TIMOTHY 6:6

COLESLAW (CABBAGE SALAD)

Shred cabbage and carrots quite fine. Add onion and pepper. (These may be prepared several hours ahead of time and refrigerated in tight container.) Prepare following dressing: ⅓ cup salad dressing, ½ teaspoon prepared mustard, 1 teaspoon vinegar, 1 tablespoon sugar, ½ teaspoon salt, dash pepper. Mix well and serve chilled.

½ small head cabbage
1 medium-sized carrot
1 teaspoon diced onion
1 small wedge green
   pepper, minced

FRUIT SALAD

1 can mandarin orange
  sections, drained
1 small can white
  grapes, drained
3 bananas, sliced
2 apples, chopped

Mix all ingredients well. Toss with ½ cup powdered sugar and let stand in refrigerator an hour or two before serving.

CRAB LOUIS

Dressing
1 cup mayonnaise
⅓ cup whipping cream
¼ cup chili sauce
1 tablespoon chopped
  green pepper
⅓ cup green onion and
  tops, chopped
1 tablespoon lemon
  juice
Salad
1 large head lettuce
2½ cups crab meat
2 large tomatoes
3 hard boiled eggs,
  divided

Mix first six ingredients thoroughly and chill.

Arrange lettuce on 4 large salad plates. Clean crab meat and arrange on top of the lettuce. Circle with thin wedges of the tomato and egg. Pour ⅓ cup of the dressing over each salad. Top with remaining crab meat and a dollop of mayonnaise. Serves 4.

CHICKEN SALAD

2 cups chicken, chopped
2 teaspoons minced
  onion
5 tablespoons minced
  celery
¼ cup ripe olives,
  chopped
1 teaspoon lemon juice
⅓ cup mayonnaise
2 tablespoons chopped
  parsley

Mix all ingredients and fill cocktail puffs, or serve on a bed of lettuce.

COTTAGE CHEESE SALAD

4 lettuce leaves
2 cups cottage cheese
4 pear halves, peach
  halves, pineapple
  rings, or spiced apple
  rings
Mayonnaise

Arrange lettuce leaves on small salad plates. Top each with ½ cup cottage cheese, fruit, and a dab of mayonnaise. Serve crisp and cold. Serves 4.

BROCCOLI-CAULIFLOWER SALAD

1 bunch fresh broccoli
1 head cauliflower
2 green onions
Marinade
½ cup margarine
⅓ cup red wine vinegar
⅓ cup oil
⅓ cup sugar
½ teaspoon salt

Break or cut ingredients into small pieces. Mix marinade ingredients and pour over the vegetables. Place in covered dish in refrigerator overnight.

DRESSINGS
EASY FRENCH DRESSING

Mix ingredients well. Store in refrigerator for use at your convenience. Merely shake jar well before using. Makes almost a quart of dressing.

1 cup salad oil
⅓ cup vinegar
1 cup sugar
1 teaspoon salt
1 teaspoon pepper
1 tablespoon prepared mustard
1 cup catsup
1 small garlic bud, diced fine
1 tablespoon grated onion

THOUSAND ISLAND DRESSING

Mix ingredients well and store in refrigerator.

1 cup mayonnaise
½ cup chili sauce
1 dill pickle, minced
¼ cup celery, minced
1 small onion, minced
2 hard-cooked eggs, cut fine
1 small green pepper, minced

MAYONNAISE

Beat together all ingredients. Add 4 cups salad oil a few drops at a time, beating constantly, and ¼ cup additional vinegar. Store in airtight container and refrigerate.

4 egg yolks
¼ cup honey
⅛ teaspoon paprika
¼ cup vinegar

Sandwiches

SEVENTEEN

GRILLED CHEESE SANDWICH
Butter two slices bread for each sandwich. Place one slice of processed cheese on unbuttered side; top with other slice, buttered side up. Place on heated griddle or in electric skillet on medium heat. Cook slowly until one side is brown, turn to brown other side. Serve at once.

EGG SALAD SANDWICH
Cook 3 or 4 eggs until hard. Chop fine and mix with 1 teaspoon finely grated onion. Mix with mayonnaise, salt, and pepper. Spread.

CREAMED DRIED BEEF ON TOAST
Melt 3 tablespoons butter in skillet or saucepan. Add one small package dried beef, shredded. Brown lightly, stirring constantly. Add 1½ tablespoons flour. Add 2 cups milk, pouring slowly while stirring. (Use more or less milk to make the cream sauce the consistency you desire.) Spoon over squares of hot buttered toast and serve immediately. Serves 4.

RIBBON SANDWICHES
Grind chicken, ham, and eggs separately. To each, add mayonnaise and onion to taste. Use enough mayonnaise to make it easy to spread. Set aside.

Soften cheese and thin with a little milk. Make this of spreading consistency also. Set aside.

Cut crusts from bread and arrange in stacks of 4. Using the white bread, lay 4 slices of bread side by side and spread with chicken mixture. Then top with 4 slices of brown bread and spread with egg mixture. Top with another row of white bread slices and spread with ham mixture. Top with brown bread slices. Then "frost" with the cheese mixture, covering top and all sides. You may want to use more cream cheese if you like it thick and "cheesey." When all sides, ends, and top are covered with the cheese, cover with plastic wrap and refrigerate overnight if possible. It will cut more easily if it is quite cool. An electric knife works very well. Cut into slices and serve.

Oh, how grateful and thankful I am to the Lord because he is so good. I will sing praise to the name of the Lord who is above all lords.
PSALM 7:17

2 cups cooked chicken
2 cups baked ham
8 eggs, boiled
2 cups mayonnaise
¼ cup onion, ground
2 8-ounce packages
    cream cheese
8 slices white bread
8 slices brown bread

109

HAM SALAD SANDWICH

There are several ways to make a ham salad sandwich. Grind boiled or baked ham in food grinder along with a sweet pickle and mix with mayonnaise. Or grind minced ham, leftover ring bologna, or a couple of wieners and mix with the above ingredients. One or two chopped hard-cooked eggs make a tasty addition and stretch the meat. May be used for closed or open-faced sandwiches.

TUNA SALAD SANDWICH

Combine 1 can tuna with 1 chopped hard-cooked egg and a finely chopped sweet pickle. Mix with mayonnaise to spreading consistency and spread on bread.

The path of the godly leads to life. So why fear death?
PROVERBS 12:28

Sauces and Soups

EIGHTEEN

SAUCES

HOT SAUCE FOR STEAK OR CHICKEN

Mix all ingredients together in quart jar. Pour over chicken or steak and bake 1 hour at 350°, or until tender.

2 cups tomato juice
1 small onion
3 tablespoons vinegar
1/3 cup brown sugar
1 tablespoon salt
1/8 teaspoon Tabasco
  sauce
1 tablespoon dry
  mustard

GLAZE FOR HAM

Mix ingredients together in a small bowl. Spread over ham the last 40 minutes of baking.

1 cup firmly packed
  brown sugar
1 tablespoon flour
1 teaspoon dry mustard
2 tablespoons vinegar

RAISIN SAUCE

Combine dry ingredients. Combine liquids; pour gradually into dry ingredients and stir until smooth. Place over low heat and cook until thick, stirring constantly. Serve with hot ham or pork.

1/2 cup brown sugar
1 teaspoon dry mustard
1 tablespoon flour
1 1/2 cups water
2 tablespoons lemon
  juice
2 tablespoons vinegar
1/4 teaspoon grated
  lemon rind
1/3 cup raisins

BARBECUE SAUCE

Combine in saucepan and simmer 25 minutes, stirring often to prevent scorching. May be used for basting of chicken while barbecuing on outdoor grill. To use on frying chicken baked in oven, baste chicken before putting in oven, then baste every 15 minutes, turning chicken as it bakes in moderate oven 1 hour or until well done. It is also good spooned over chops which are then covered tightly and baked for an hour. Keeps well in refrigerator.

2 bottles catsup
2 stalks celery, diced
1 small onion, diced
2 cloves garlic, diced
1 pound butter
1 bottle barbecue sauce
  (1 pound, 2 ounces)
1 tablespoon chili
  powder
1/4 green pepper, minced
1 pint white vinegar

WHITE SAUCE

Melt 1 tablespoon butter in saucepan over low heat. While stirring constantly, add 1 tablespoon flour. Slowly add 1 cup milk and stir until thick and smooth. If a thinner white sauce is desired, increase the amount of milk, or decrease for a thicker white sauce. Add ¼ teaspoon salt and a dash of pepper.

If you are tired of the outlook, try the UP-look.

SOUPS

POTATO SOUP

Dice 2 medium-sized potatoes; add 1 small onion, diced. Cover with water and cook slowly 15 to 20 minutes, or until vegetables are tender and liquid barely covers vegetables. Add 1 quart milk and 1 tablespoon butter. Salt and pepper. Heat to boiling point and serve hot. Serves 2.

Mixed up? Try getting things straightened up with the Lord . . . and he will make your paths straight.

BEAN SOUP

Boil ham bone (or 1 cup baked ham, diced) in 3 cups water 30 minutes. Wash and drain 1 pound dry beans. Add beans and 1 small diced onion to ham; cover with water and bring to boil. Turn heat down and simmer 3 to 4 hours, or until beans are tender, adding just enough water to keep beans covered. They absorb quite a bit of water, so check every half hour or so to be sure they don't cook dry and burn.

CHILI CON CARNE

1 can red chili beans
1 medium onion, diced
1 pound ground beef
3 tablespoons fat
1 No. 2 can tomatoes
1½ teaspoons salt
1 tablespoon chili
   powder
1 small green pepper,
   chopped

Brown onion, meat, and green pepper in fat. Add tomatoes and seasoning. Simmer slowly 1 hour, adding water if needed. Add beans, juice and all, and simmer 15 minutes longer. Serves 4.

VEGETABLE SOUP

Cover soup bone or ½ pound stewing beef with water, add 1 teaspoon salt, and simmer for 2 hours. Add 2 cups green beans, 2 sliced carrots, 1 small onion, and ½ small head of cabbage, coarsely chopped. Add enough tomato juice to cover all. Cook slowly for an additional 30 minutes or until vegetables are tender. For extra flavor, add 1 tablespoon of cream just before serving.

OYSTER STEW

Heat either fresh or canned oysters in their liquor (for fresh oysters, add ½ cup water). Add 2 quarts milk to 1 pint oysters. Add ⅛ teaspoon pepper, ½ teaspoon salt, and 2 tablespoons butter. Bring just to boiling point, stirring occasionally. Serve piping hot with small oyster crackers. Serves 4.

SPLIT PEA SOUP

Soak peas in 2 quarts water overnight. Bring to boil, add onions, bacon or ham, and celery. Cover and cook on slow boil 2 to 2½ hours, or until peas are tender and liquid is cooked down. Season. For a creamed soup, put through sieve and add water or milk to desired thickness.

¾ cup dried split peas
1 medium onion
2 slices bacon or a ham bone
2 stalks celery, chopped fine
Salt and pepper

Trix with Mixes

NINETEEN

STRIPE IT RICH CAKE

Prepare cake mix as directed and pour into a greased and floured 9″ x 13″ cake pan. Bake as instructed.

When baked, remove from oven and immediately poke holes in cake with straw or utensil handle. After holes are made, combine pudding mix and powdered sugar in a large bowl. Gradually add milk. Beat on low speed not more than 1 minute. Quickly, before pudding sets, pour ½ the pudding mix over warm cake into the holes.

Allow the remaining pudding to thicken slightly, then spoon it over the cake swirling to "frost" the cake. Chill and store in the refrigerator until used.

1 package (2 layer size) cake mix, any flavor
2 packages (4 serving size) Jell-O Brand Instant Pudding, any flavor
1 cup powdered sugar
1 cup cold milk

ED LAUER'S DUMP CAKE

Spread each item as listed above evenly into a 9″ x 13″ baking pan. Bake 1 hour at 350°. (Place pan on cookie sheet as it may boil over.) Best when served hot.

1 16-ounce can apple pie mix
1 16-ounce can crushed pineapple
1 box yellow or white cake mix
2 sticks margarine or butter, cut into patties
1 cup shredded coconut
1 cup chopped nuts

JUNE'S CHOCOLATE TORTE DESSERT

Mix first three ingredients and spread on bottom of 9″ x 13″ pan and bake for 15 minutes at 350°. Remove from oven.

Mix next three ingredients and spread over cooled crust. Reserve about 1½ cups.

Mix pudding according to package instructions, but *decrease* milk by ½ cup. Spread vanilla pudding over the cheese mixture and spread chocolate pudding over the vanilla pudding. Top with remaining whipped cream cheese mixture. Garnish with chopped nuts or shaved dark chocolate.

1 cup chopped nuts
1 cup flour
½ cup butter
1 8-ounce package cream cheese
1½ cups whipped cream
1½ cups powdered sugar
1 large box instant vanilla pudding mix
1 large box instant chocolate pudding mix

BANANA BUNDT CAKE

⅓ cup margarine
1 package coconut-pecan frosting mix
1 cup instant oatmeal
1 cup sour cream
4 eggs
1 cup bananas, mashed
1 2-layer yellow cake mix

Melt margarine and stir in frosting mix. Add oatmeal and blend until crumbly. In a large bowl, combine eggs, sour cream, and bananas. Beat until smooth. Add cake mix and beat for one minute at high speed. Pour ⅓ of the crumb mixture into well-greased and floured bundt pan. Pour ⅓ of the cake mixture into pan and repeat in thirds until all is used. Bake for an hour at 350°. Cool for 5 minutes and remove from pan.

NORMA'S STRAWBERRY CAKE

1 cup sliced strawberries
½ cup sugar
1 3-ounce package strawberry Jell-O
1½ cups miniature marshmallows
1 2-layer white cake mix

Combine strawberries, sugar, and Jell-O. Set aside.

Generously grease a 9″ x 13″ pan and sprinkle the marshmallows over the bottom. Mix the cake according to directions on box and pour over marshmallows. Spoon the strawberry mixture on top and bake at 350° for 40 to 45 minutes. Serve warm or cold with ice cream or whipped cream.

CHOCOLATE PIE SUPREME

1 package chocolate instant pudding mix
1 package vanilla instant pudding mix
2 cups milk
2 cups chocolate ice cream
1 baked pie crust

Mix all ingredients, having softened the ice cream to make it "mixable" and pour into baked pie crust. Refrigerate overnight and serve with whipped cream.

PINEAPPLE CAKE

1 large can crushed pineapple
1 2-layer yellow cake mix
½ pound butter

In a 9″ x 13″ pan, spread the crushed pineapple over the bottom. Then sprinkle the cake mix over the pineapple and then top this with the butter, sliced very thin and layered on the top. Bake at 350° for 30 to 40 minutes. Serve with ice cream or whipped cream.

LEMON-POPPY SEED LOAF

1 lemon cake mix
1 cup hot water
½ cup oil
¼ cup poppy seeds
1 instant lemon pudding mix
4 eggs

Beat ingredients together in a large bowl with an electric mixer. Pour into 2 large or 3 small greased and floured loaf pans. Bake 1 hour at 325°.

À la Mode—To top with ice cream.

Antipasto—(ahn-te-*pahs*-toh) Assorted appetizers of fish, cold meats, vegetables, or relish.

Aspic—A gelatin made from concentrated meat, fish, or vegetable stock.

Au Gratin—(aw-*grah*-tin) To cover with browned bread crumbs, often using butter and cheese.

Bake—To cook by dry heat in closed oven, generally called roasting when applied to meats.

Barbecue—To cook meat on grill or spit over coals or open flame, usually basting with seasoned sauce.

Baste—To spoon or pour liquid over meats or other foods while cooking, to enhance the flavor or keep from drying out.

Batter—A flour and liquid mixture, or other ingredients such as eggs, thin enough to pour; for example, cake batter, pancake batter, batter for coating foods for deep fat frying.

Beat—To lift and turn mixture over and over wth a swift motion, using egg beater or electric mixer.

Blanch—To place quickly into boiling water to loosen skin from tomatoes or fruits or to plunge into boiling water, then quickly into cold water.

Bisque—A thick French soup made from shellfish, bird, or rabbit.

Boil—To heat liquid to a point where bubbles break and roll on the surface.

Bouillon—(boo-yawn) A clear meat broth.

Bouillon Cube—Cube of concentrated and dehydrated broth, liquid to be added; as beef or chicken bouillon cubes.

Braise—To cook meat, covered, in a small amount of liquid.

Bread—To coat or cover with liquid (usually slightly beaten eggs) and then roll in bread or other crumbs to coat.

Brine—A salt and water mixture used to preserve or pickle.

Brown—To pan fry, bake, broil, or roast until food takes on a brown color.

Broth—A liquid extracted by cooking food, usually in water on top of stove.

Canapé—(ca-na-*pay*) Small, bite-sized piece of pastry, toasted or fried bread, or crackers topped with cheese, meat, or seafood.

Candy—To cook a second time in sugar or syrup.

Caramelize—To melt white or brown sugar to a golden brown syrup over very low heat.

Chop—To cut with a sharp knife into pieces or chunks; also a certain cut of meat, as a pork chop, lamb chop, etc.

Chowder—A cream soup usually made with clams, potatoes, onions, or other vegetables.

Cocktail—A beverage; a highly seasoned food designed to be an appetizer before a meal; may be used as a first course.

Compote—Fruit cooked in heavy syrup so as to retain shape; also a serving dish used for candies or fruits.

117

Condiment—A seasoning.

Confectioners' Sugar—A white, powder-fine sugar used in icings and commonly called powdered sugar or icing sugar.

Consommé—A strong, clear soup or bouillon.

Cream—To beat together until mixture forms a smooth, creamy substance.

Creole—(*kree*-ohl) Well-seasoned foods containing tomatoes, green peppers, onions and other spices.

Crêpe—A very thin, crisp pancake.

Croquette—Very finely ground meat or fish mixed with white sauce, shaped, dipped in beaten eggs, and rolled in crumbs before browning in fat.

Crumb—To break into very small pieces; to coat with crumbs.

Cut In—To blend or mix fat into flour usually using a pastry blender or knife; to distribute solid fat.

Curry—A highly spiced East Indian sauce (available in powder form) to give flavor to stews, sauces, and main dishes.

Cutlet—Small slice of meat from ribs or legs to be fried or broiled, such as pork cutlet, veal cutlet, etc.

Devil—To season, as in deviled eggs (hard-cook eggs, remove yolks, season, restuff whites).

Devil's Food—Usually referring to a type of chocolate cake.

Dice—To cut into small cubes.

Dough—A flour and liquid mixture (may be other ingredients), not baked, thick enough to roll out and knead.

Dredge—To sprinkle liberally with flour.

Drippings—Moisture (juice or fat) collected in bottom of roaster pan.

Eclair—A small, oblong cake containing a filling, usually covered with sugar or chocolate icing.

Entrée—(*on*-tray) A dish served between heavy courses or before the main course; or may be the main course.

Escallop—Same as scallop.

Filet Mignon—(fill-*lay* min-*yahn*) A choice, thick slice of beef from the tenderloin, usually broiled.

Filet or Fillet—A long, thin boneless strip of meat from fish or veal.

Fondant—A type of candy made from confectioner's sugar.

Fondue—A cheese and egg dish.

Fold In—To turn over and over gently, cutting carefully through mixture and slipping the spoon across the bottom of the bowl at each turn.

French Fry—To cook in hot fat deep enough to more than cover the food.

Fricassee—(*frick*-a-see) A dish made of chicken or rabbit cut into pieces, stewed, and then fried or stewed in gravy or sauce.

Fritter—Small cake similar to doughnuts, but with meat or fruit cooked in the center.

Frizzle—To cook on hot coals until crisp.

Fromage—A sour milk cheese dish.

Fry—To cook in hot fat in pan on top of stove.

Garnish—To decorate with bits of other food for color or taste.

Glacé—To cover with icing.

Glaze—To coat food with sugar icing, syrup, or jelly.

Goulash—A Hungarian meat dish made with tomatoes, macaroni, spices, and meat.

Grate—To shred food.

Grill—To broil on a grill over hot coals; to cook by direct heat.

Grind—To pulverize or cut extremely fine in food chopper.

Herbs—Plants used for seasonings or garnishes.

Hors d'Oeuvres—Dainty, attractive appetizers of hot or cold foods, varied in shape.

Jambalaya—Meat or lobster served with creole sauce.

Jell—To cool gelatin mixture until it is semi-firm or beyond the pouring stage.

Julienne—To cut food into shoe-stringlike strips.

Kippered—Salted, smoke-dried, cured fish as salmon or herring.

Knead—To work into a mass, as bread dough, folding and pressing well with the heel of the hand.

Kosher—Applied to food prepared according to Hebrew custom; a Russian type of dill pickle.

Lard—To insert strips of fat into uncooked meat for flavor and moisture. Also, a shortening made from animal fat.

Level—To even off in measuring with the aid of a straight knife.

Leavening—Yeast, baking powder, or soda added to batter to produce light, edible products.

Liquor—The liquid in which canned food is packed, or in which foods are cooked.

Marbling—To mix two different colors or flavors gently to produce a marble-like appearance in cakes and cookies; small streaks of white fat throughout beef of high quality.

Marinade—A mixture of oils and acids used to give flavor, or to tenderize meats and vegetables.

Marinate—To soak food in an oil and acid mixture for flavor.

Meringue—A pie or pudding topping made of stiffly beaten egg white and sugar, then browned in oven.

Mince—To chop into minute pieces.

Minestrone—A thick Italian soup made with meat stock and vegetables.

Neopolitan—Dessert made of layers of ice cream and ices, frozen and sliced for serving.

Nougat—A candy or confection containing almonds, pistachio nuts, and sugar paste. Occasionally fruit is added.

Pan Broil—To cook uncovered in a hot, lightly greased skillet, pouring off fat as it melts.

Pan Fry—To cook in skillet in small amount of fat.

Parboil—To partially cook in boiling water.

Pare—To cut off outer skin or covering.

Parfait—(par-*fay*) A frozen dessert of whipped cream and a syrup cooked with eggs and flavoring; ice cream and fruit mixture frozen in tall, stemmed glasses.

Pasta—A paste of dough such as spaghetti or macaroni usually added to soup.

Patty—A small pie; a mixture of foods formed into a round flat shape and fried.

Petit—Very young tender peas; small or new.

Petit four—Small fancy cake for tea, usually completely iced.

Pfeffernuesse—Pepper nuts; small, spiced German cookies.

Pot Liquor—The liquid in which vegetables have been cooked.

Pot Roast—Large piece of meat cooked by braising rather than by baking or roasting.

Puree—Cooked vegetable or fruit which has been pressed through a fine sieve.

Powdered sugar—Same as confectioner's sugar.

Ragout—Dish of stewed and highly seasoned meat.

Ravioli—An Italian noodle dough spread with meat or vegetable as a filling, the dough folded over, and cooked or baked in tomato sauce.

Relish—A variety of raw vegetables cut into various shapes.

Rice—To press cooked vegetables through a fine "ricer."

Roast—To cook, usually in oven, but sometimes over an open fire.

Roll—To spread thin with a rolling pin; or the act of taking hold of one side of rolled out dough and rolling it against itself to form a larger roll.

Rosette—A pastry formed by dipping a special fancy-shaped iron into batter and then into hot fat. Rosettes are served with creamed foods as a main course, or as a dessert with ice cream.

Roux—A mixture of flour and butter used to thicken sauces and soups.

Sauté—To brown quickly in skillet in small amount of fat.

Scald—To heat to a temperature just below the boiling point; to pour boiling water over.

Scallion—Green onion with small or no bulb.

Scallop—To bake food with buttered bread or cracker crumbs in deep dish in the oven.

Score—To cut gashes with a sharp knife part way through food.

Sear—To brown surface quickly in hot skillet.

Season—To spice moderately.

Sherbet—A frozen dessert of fruit juice, sugar, and milk, usually with little cream or butterfat content.

Shortening—An ingredient for making bread or pastry tender, such as lard, butter, margarine.

Shred—To tear or cut into small pieces.

Sift—To put dry ingredients through a sieve.

Simmer—To cook in liquid just below the boiling point.

Skewer—A metal or wood pin used to fasten meat for cooking.

Smorgasbord—Swedish appetizer course consisting of a wide variety of foods served buffet style.

Soufflé—(soo-*flay*) A baked dish made light by using whipped egg whites.

Spice—An aromatic herb or other substance used for seasoning or flavoring.

Steam—To cook in small amount of boiling water in covered container.

Steep—To allow a substance to stand in liquid just below boiling point.

Sterilize—To destroy germs by boiling in water, or by using dry heat.

Stew—To simmer foods slowly in small quantity of water for a long time.

Tabasco—A long, red, very hot pepper used chiefly in sauces.

Tartar Sauce—Sauce with a mayonnaise base and finely chopped onion, pickle, or other seasonings, usually eaten with seafood.

Truss—To fasten into position with skewers and twine, as for fowl.

Whip—To beat rapidly to incorporate air to produce volume, as in whipped cream, egg whites, or whipped gelatin.

RECIPE
INDEX

121